More life science titles in the **Explore Your World!** series

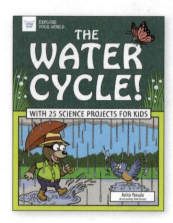
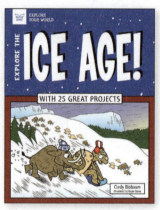

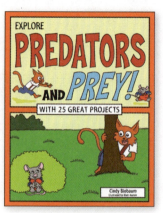

Check out more titles at www.nomadpress.net

Nomad Press
A division of Nomad Communications
10 9 8 7 6 5 4 3 2 1
Copyright © 2019 by Nomad Press. All rights reserved.
No part of this book may be reproduced in any form without permission in writing from
the publisher, except by a reviewer who may quote brief passages in a review or **for limited educational use**.
The trademark "Nomad Press" and the Nomad Press logo are trademarks of Nomad Communications, Inc.

This book was manufactured by Versa Press,
East Peoria, Illinois
August 2019, Job #J18-13168

ISBN Softcover: 978-1-61930-809-1
ISBN Hardcover: 978-1-61930-806-0

Educational Consultant, Marla Conn

Questions regarding the ordering of this book should be addressed to
Nomad Press
2456 Christian St.
White River Junction, VT 05001
www.nomadpress.net

Printed in the United States of America.

CONTENTS

Introduction . . . 1
What's Under Your Skin?

Chapter 1 . . . 10
Bone Basics

Chapter 2 . . . 26
Head and Neck Above the Rest

Chapter 3 . . . 42
Torsos to Tails

Chapter 4 . . . 54
Out on a Limb

Chapter 5 . . . 66
Give Yourself a Hand!

Glossary * Metric Conversions
Resources * Essential Questions * Index

Interested in primary sources? Look for this icon. Use a smartphone or tablet app to scan the QR code and explore more! Photos are also primary sources because a photograph takes a picture at the moment something happens.

You can find a list of URLs on the Resources page. Try searching the internet with the Keyword Prompts to find other helpful sources.

KEYWORD PROMPTS

skulls and skeletons

SKULLS AND SKELETONS

500 MILLION YEARS AGO: The first "bones" appear in jawless, fishlike animals.

125,000 YEARS AGO: Early humans start using animal bones as tools.

40,000 YEARS AGO: Early Europeans make flutes from vulture and other bird bones.

C. 3000 BCE: Ancient Egyptians write about medical treatments for bones.

C. 400 BCE: A Greek doctor named Hippocrates writes about treating dislocated and broken bones with bandages and splints.

C. 315 BCE: A Greek scientist named Aristotle compares, describes, and classifies about 540 different kinds of animals. He writes that humans are the only animals to walk on two legs and have knees that bend forward.

C. 180 CE: A Greek doctor named Galen dissects dogs, pigs, and monkeys and studies a human skeleton. He gives a good description of the human skull and muscles.

C. 1511: Italian artist and inventor Leonardo da Vinci studies skeletons. He realizes that the part of the skeleton labelled as a knee on most animals is actually the ankle.

1543: Belgian anatomist Andreas Vesalius publishes an important anatomy book.

1730s: British surgeon John Hunter discovers that bones are living tissue.

TIMELINE

1736: Bonesetter Sally Mapp is paid to live in Epsom, England, to treat injured people and animals. She moves fractured or dislocated bones back into their proper places so they can heal correctly.

1749–1788: French naturalist Louis Jean Marie Daubenton compares the anatomy of 82 quadrupeds plus many other animals for *Buffon's Natural History*.

1780: Swiss doctor Jean-Andre Venel opens the first clinic for treating skeletal deformities in children.

1868: For the first time ever, a dinosaur skeleton is put on display in the Academy of Natural Science Museum in Philadelphia, Pennsylvania.

1875: Welsh surgeon Hugh Owen Thomas invents a splint to keep the ends of bones together and motionless.

1895: German physicist Wilhelm Conrad Roentgen discovers X-rays.

1956: Dr. E. Donnall Thomas performs the first successful bone marrow transplant in Cooperstown, New York, to help a patient fight leukemia.

1988: American Jeannie Peeper starts a foundation to raise funds so scientists can study the rare condition that makes her body grow a second skeleton.

2018: Researchers are experimenting with putting stem cells taken from a person's own fat cells onto their damaged bones to help the bones heal faster.

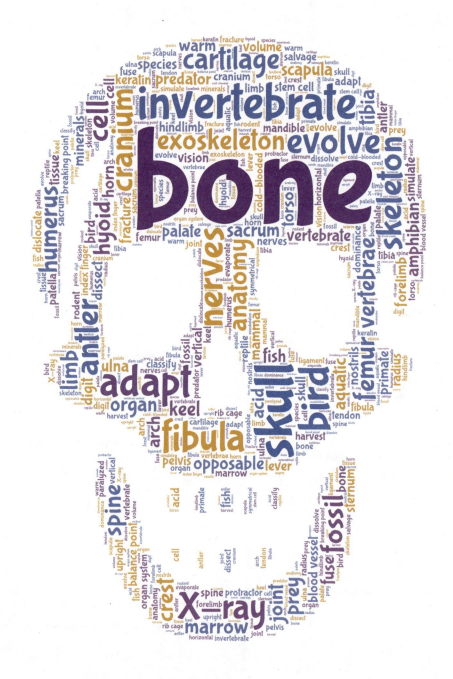

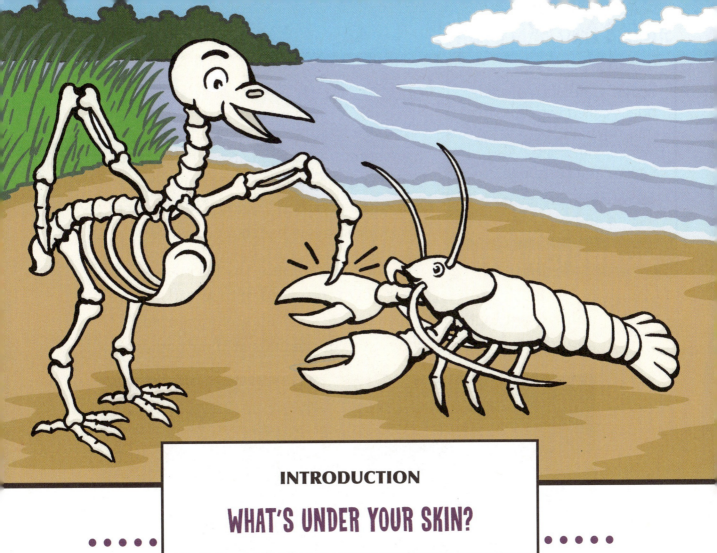

INTRODUCTION

WHAT'S UNDER YOUR SKIN?

This book is about hard stuff! But not stuff that's hard to understand. Instead, this book is about objects that are as hard as rocks. In fact, these objects are made of many of the same things as some rocks!

This book is about **bones**! Reach your arm around and feel the middle of your back. Touch the hard bumps that start where your head and neck meet. Feel the bumps all the way down to your bottom.

WORDS TO KNOW

bone: hard, connective tissue in an animal's body that provides support, protection and a place for muscle attachment. Blood is produced in some bones.

SKULLS AND SKELETONS!

> **spine:** a line of connected bones called vertebrae that runs down the back of an animal with bones. Also known as a backbone.
>
> **vertebrate:** any animal that has a spine.
>
> **WORDS TO KNOW**

You are feeling your **spine**! Animals that have spines are called **vertebrates**. Your spine and the spines of most vertebrates are made of bones. That is why another word for spine is backbone.

In most vertebrates, the backbones go clear down to the tip of their tails. For animals without tails—such as frogs, gorillas, chimpanzees, and people—the backbones stop at the ends of their bodies.

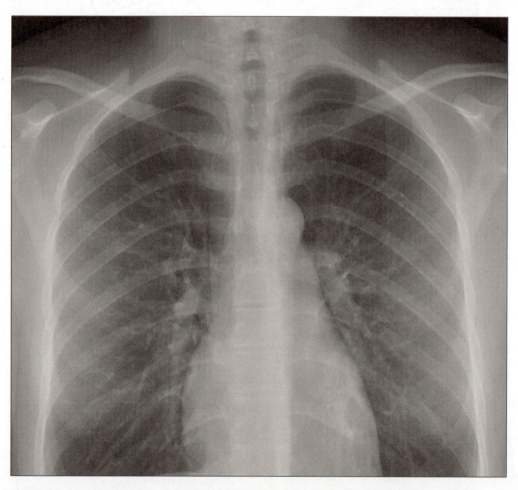

A CHEST X-RAY SHOWING A HUMAN SPINE. CAN YOU ALSO SPOT THE RIBS?
CREDIT: MIKAEL HÄGGSTRÖM (CC0 1.0)

WHAT'S UNDER YOUR SKIN?

Vertebrate animals include mammals, birds, reptiles, amphibians, and fish. Mammals and birds are warm-blooded animals, while reptiles, amphibians, and fish are cold-blooded animals.

JOBS FOR BONES

Of course, vertebrate animals have more bones than just backbones! Flat bones, such as the ones that make the skull and rib cage, protect important body parts—the head and chest. The flat bones in shoulders and hips work to join parts together.

The round, long bones in arms, legs, wings, hands, fins, and feet have muscles on them. These muscles help animals stand, sit, grab, walk, jump, swim, and fly.

You even have tiny bones that help you hear. Another one helps you talk!

mammal: a warm-blooded vertebrate animal, such as a human, dog, or cat. Mammals feed milk to their young and usually have hair or fur covering most of their skin.

bird: a warm-blooded vertebrate animal with feathers covering most of its body. Birds hatch from eggs and most have wings that help them fly. Turkeys, ducks, and penguins are birds.

reptile: a cold-blooded vertebrate animal such as a snake, lizard, alligator, or turtle, that has a spine, lays eggs, has scales or horny plates, and breathes air.

amphibian: a cold-blooded vertebrate animal, such as a toad, frog, or salamander. Amphibians live on land and in the water.

fish: a vertebrate animal that lives in water, uses gills to breathe, and usually hatches from an egg. Fish do not have any limbs and most have scales. Goldfish, eels, and sharks are fish.

warm-blooded: an animal that can create its own body heat.

cold-blooded: an animal whose body temperature changes with the air or water temperature around it.

skull: the bone case that holds in place and protects the brain and other parts of an animal's head.

WORDS TO KNOW

SKULLS AND SKELETONS!

cartilage: elastic, flexible tissue in the body.

skeleton: the framework of bones that supports the body of a vertebrate animal.

minerals: the natural ingredients that are part of all things on Earth. Salt and calcium are examples of minerals.

cell: the basic part of a living thing. Cells are so small they can be seen only with a microscope. There are billions of cells in most living things.

hyoid: the bone in your throat at the base of your tongue.

WORDS TO KNOW

DID YOU KNOW?

The spines in some vertebrates are made of cartilage. This is softer and more flexible than bone. You can read more about cartilage in Chapter 1.

Each bone has a special shape and is in the right place to do its job. All the bones together make a skeleton. Your bones have some hidden jobs as well. Your blood is made inside the big, round bones in your arms and legs. That way, when you scrape your knee and some blood leaks out, you have plenty of new blood to replace it.

Your bones also store the minerals you need to be healthy and grow. Bones are filled with minerals, just as rocks are! Minerals are non-living ingredients that come from the earth. Your cells need minerals to do their jobs, such as making bone, muscle, and blood.

BONE ON THE LOOSE!

There is only one bone in your body that is not connected to any other bone. It is found in your throat and is called the hyoid bone. The hyoid helps keep your tongue rooted in the back of your throat. It also does a lot of work when you swallow!

WHAT'S UNDER YOUR SKIN?

You get the minerals your cells need from the food you eat. You don't have to eat each mineral every day, because your bones store some of them for you!

Animals without backbones are called invertebrates. Invertebrates include worms, insects, spiders, clams, lobsters, jellyfish, and many others. Some of these have a type of skeleton on the outside of their bodies. Think of a beetle. It has a hard shell that acts as a protector around its body. This is called an exoskeleton.

In *Skulls and Skeletons!* you'll discover lots of information about the bones that make up skulls and skeletons. You'll also learn how bones are made, how they are used, and how to keep your bones healthy.

What about the bones of other vertebrates? How are they similar to ours? How are they different? What about the exoskeletons of some invertebrates? We'll take a look at these, too. Let's move those eyes in their sockets and get reading!

> **invertebrate:** an animal that does not have bones inside its body.
>
> **exoskeleton:** a hard shell or cover on the outside of some invertebrates that provides support and protection.
>
> ## WORDS TO KNOW

The world's smallest vertebrate is a tiny frog. It is so small that three or four of them could fit on a dime! Take a look!

KEYWORD PROMPTS

smallest vertebrate, tiny frog

SKULLS AND SKELETONS!

GOOD SCIENCE PRACTICES

Every good scientist keeps a science journal. In the first activity, you will make a notebook to use as your science journal. Each chapter in this book begins with a question to help guide your exploration of skulls and skeletons. Write down your first guess, and then add ideas, observations, and comparisons as you read the chapter.

 INVESTIGATE!

What do you think are the largest bones in your body?

Scientific Method Worksheet
Question: What are we trying to find out? What problem are we trying to solve?
Research: What information is already known?
Hypothesis/Prediction: What do we think the answer will be?
Equipment: What supplies are we using?
Method: What are the steps we are following?
Results: What happened and why?
What next? Do the results change when I do something different? What else can I do to explore this idea?

Scientists use the scientific method to keep their experiments organized. By recording what they think, do, and see, scientists can prove their results. Many of the projects in this book tell you to use a scientific method worksheet like the one shown here. By using your journal, doing the projects, and following the scientific method, you can answer the questions with confidence!

PROJECT!

SKULLS AND SKELETONS SCIENCE JOURNAL

SUPPLIES
* 5 to 10 sheets unlined copy paper
* hole punch
* 10 to 20 sheets lined paper
* 3 ring binder or folder
* art supplies

Good scientists keep track of what they think and do. This helps them remember things. Journals also help them share and compare what they have learned with other scientists. Create a science journal for the projects you do in this book. You can also include other projects and ideas.

1 Put all the unlined sheets in a neat stack. Make sure all the edges are even. Use the hole punch to make holes in them.

2 Place all the lined sheets in a neat stack. Make sure all the edges are even. If needed, use the hole punch to make holes along one edge.

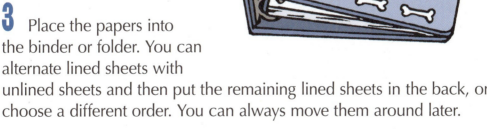

3 Place the papers into the binder or folder. You can alternate lined sheets with unlined sheets and then put the remaining lined sheets in the back, or choose a different order. You can always move them around later.

4 Use the art supplies to decorate the front cover. You might want to copy the scientific method onto the first page. This way, it is easy to find and look at when you start a new project.

PROJECT!

ANY BODY?

Your skeleton provides support for your body. There are not many realistic vertebrate animal toys out there. Most toys are either stuffed and soft, or plastic and hard. This makes them great models for what we might be like if we did not have backbones!

SUPPLIES
* journal and pencil
* stuffed animal or doll
* hard plastic toy (doll, animal, or action figure)
* 4 to 5 heavy books

1 Make a chart like this in your skulls and skeletons journal.

Toy	Is it bendable? Yes/No	How many books can it hold and still keep its shape?	How many different ways can it stand or sit?
Stuffed toy	Forward: _____ Backward: _____ Sideways: _____		
Hard plastic toy	Forward: _____ Backward: _____ Sideways: _____		
Me	Forward: _____ Backward: _____ Sideways: _____		

PROJECT!

2 Put each model through the tests explained in the chart. Try these tests on yourself, too. Record the results. Remember, you are NOT trying to break the toy. You are just testing it.

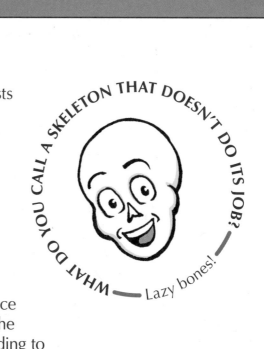

- Can you bend the model forward, backward, and to each side without breaking it?

- Put one model on the floor. Place one book on its middle. Does the model keep its shape? Keep adding to the stack, one book at a time. When the model starts to flatten, stop adding books and record the number of books used in your chart. Repeat with each model (including you!).

- Can the model stand up by itself? Sit up straight? Stand on one leg? Do a headstand? Balance on the opposite hand and knee?

THINK ABOUT IT! The stuffed toy is most like a worm, slug, or other soft-bodied animal. These animals are usually found in water or soil. They are very flexible and can squeeze into or through small places. The plastic toy is most like a beetle, crab, or other hard-shelled animal. The shells on these animals are their exoskeletons. The shells give them some protection, but make it harder for them to be flexible. Jellyfish, which live only in water, would have a plastic sandwich bag as its model!

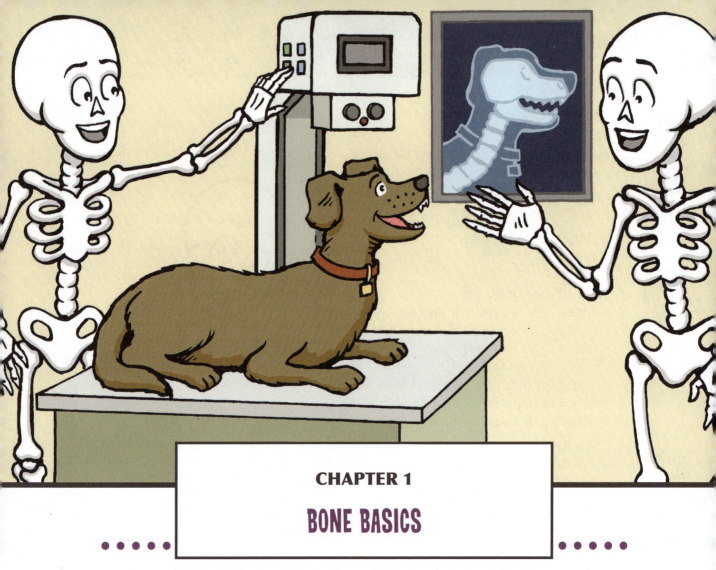

CHAPTER 1
BONE BASICS

How are the skulls and skeletons of most vertebrate animals alike? They are usually made of bones! What makes a bone, a bone? How do bones connect to each other and how can they move?

According to scientists, a bone is hardened connective tissue. What does that mean? Well, tissue in your body is made up of billions of tiny cells. About 200 different types of cells work together to do different jobs. Examples of cells include blood cells, skin cells, muscle cells, and, of course, bone cells.

? INVESTIGATE!

What would your body be like without bones?

BONE BASICS

Cells that are the same and are close together create tissue. Before a vertebrate is born, certain cells make tissue that will become bones. But the tissue starts out softer, as cartilage.

tissue: a group or mass of similar cells working together to perform common functions in plants and animals.

evolve: to gradually develop through time.

WORDS TO KNOW

You can feel cartilage by bending your ears, twitching your nose, and feeling your voice box. Cartilage gives these parts of your body the shapes you see. Cartilage is also found at the end of many bones, where it acts like a cushion to protect the ends of the bones from banging into each other.

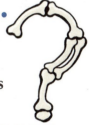

· · DID YOU KNOW? · · ·

When compared in terms of weight, pound for pound, bones are stronger than steel!

The cells in bone-making tissue take calcium and other minerals out of the blood. They put the calcium in between the cells' outer edges. The calcium sticks together and gets hard. This is one way bones change from soft tissue to hard tissue.

SHARK SURPRISE!

Sharks are some of the most ancient vertebrates still alive today. And they have very little bone in their bodies! Their backbones and the base of some of their scales have tiny pieces of bone—but most of their skeletons are made of cartilage. Most amphibian skeletons, including those of frogs, toads, and newts, are also mostly cartilage. Why do you think some animals might have *evolved* this way?

SKULLS AND SKELETONS!

> **marrow:** a jelly-like goo in the middle of some larger bones where new blood cells are made.
>
> **nerves:** living fibers that carry information between the brain and the rest of the body.
>
> **blood vessel:** a thin tube in an animal's body through which blood travels.
>
> **fuse:** to join together.
>
> ### WORDS TO KNOW

Calcium does not fill in all the spaces in all bones. The long, large bones in arms and legs have jelly-like marrow in the middle instead of calcium. Marrow is where new blood cells are formed. Bones have small holes all over them that let nerves and blood vessels go in and out.

When an animal is first born, the ends of its bones look a bit like sponges. To grow, the bone cells add new material to these ends, which are called growth plates. As the bones in the skull and at the end of some backbones grow, they fuse together. By the time a vertebrate is an adult, its body is much harder and stiffer than when it was first born.

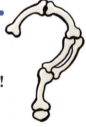

> **DID YOU KNOW?**
>
> The marrow in the human body makes about 2 million new blood cells every second! Blood cells are so small that a drop of blood contains many thousands of cells.

Even then, the bone cells don't stop working. They are always making new cells to replace old ones. If a bone gets broken or chipped, the cells work even harder to repair the damage!

STAYING SMALL

The stirrup, malleus, and stapes are the three tiny bones in your inner ear. These are the only bones in humans that never grow. The stirrup is your smallest bone. It is about the size of half a grain of rice!

BONE BASICS

GET CONNECTED

Imagine if you were made of just one bone. You wouldn't be able to bend or move very much! It also would be hard to move if your bones were not connected to each other. And bones couldn't move at all without muscles.

> **ligament:** the tough, stretchy tissue that connects two or more bones together.
>
> **tendon:** the tough, stretchy tissue that connects muscles to bones.
>
> **joint:** the movable place where two or more bones meet.
>
> ## WORDS TO KNOW

Most animal bones are connected to each other by stretchy tissue called **ligaments**. Muscles are connected to bones by tough tissue called **tendons**. The place where two or more bones meet is called a **joint**. Joints are very important. What are some joints you are using right now?

ACHILLES TENDON

There is a Greek myth about a famous warrior named Achilles. The story says when he was a baby, his mother held him by his heels and dunked him in the river Styx. The water protected his skin from all wounds—even those from swords and arrows. However, the water didn't touch his heels. He grew up to be famous for his fighting skills and for being an unbeaten soldier. But one day, another fighter shot an arrow. It hit Achilles in one of his heels, the only place he wasn't protected. Achilles died right away. Now, the tendon that attaches the calf muscles to the heel bone is named for him. Can you find your Achilles tendon?

Maxwell Day, a 14-year-old British boy, set a Guinness World Record for turning his legs so far his feet pointed backwards!

KEYWORD PROMPTS

largest external foot rotation

SKULLS AND SKELETONS!

> **torso:** the human body except the head, arms, and legs.
>
> **WORDS TO KNOW**

You can find five different kinds of joints in your body. Bend your fingers, toes, elbows, and knees. These hinge joints move mostly in just one direction. Thumbs can move in more ways because they have saddle joints where they meet the hand. Wrists can do even more because of the many bones that make up their sliding joints.

Your shoulders and hips have ball-and-socket joints to attach your arms and legs to your **torso**. These can move back and forth, up and down, and all around. Finally, at the top of your neck is a pivot joint. This lets you tilt your head up and down.

HINGE JOINT

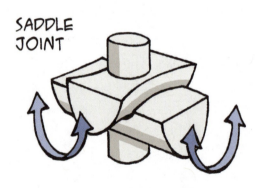

SADDLE JOINT

BALL AND SOCKET JOINT

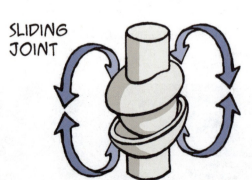

SLIDING JOINT

PIVOT JOINT

BONE BASICS

HOW BONY IS IT?

Different vertebrates have different numbers of bones. Even healthy humans don't always have the same number of bones—some have more or fewer bones than other humans!

Vertebrate Group	Animal	Average number of bones
Mammal	Adult human	206
Fish	Large fish	More than 1,500
Amphibian	Frog	159
Bird	Chicken	120
Reptile	Snake	600 to 800

BONE HISTORY

How do we know so much about bones? In some ways, we've been studying bones since early human history. Humans have always examined and used the bones of the animals they ate.

Some bones were used to make needle-like tools, hammers, and even plates. Early humans around the world used shoulder blades as hoes. Other bones were used for jewelry or art. In places without much wood, people used bones as fuel for fires.

SKULLS AND SKELETONS!

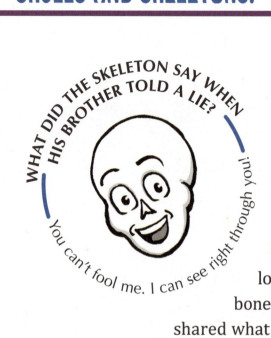

WHAT DID THE SKELETON SAY WHEN HIS BROTHER TOLD A LIE? You can't fool me. I can see right through you!

For many years in many cultures, people were not allowed to study human bones. It was considered to be witchcraft or simply disrespectful to the dead.

But healers and people who took care of the dead sometimes looked at bones. They shared what they saw and thought with other people. As time passed, people became more comfortable with the idea of learning about human bones.

DID YOU KNOW?

The Field Museum of Natural History in Chicago, Illinois, is home to Sue, a *T. rex* dinosaur. She is the most complete, best-preserved, and most expensive skeleton to be found and sold so far.

THINK ABOUT IT

After it became more acceptable to study skulls and skeletons, bone collecting became a very popular hobby. People would show off bones to families and friends or start museums. Some collectors even dug up graves or took skulls and skeletons from other countries. Now, most people realize it is important to let the skulls and skeletons of people rest in peace. What should be done with the human skulls and skeletons that are already in museums? Should there be any laws about collecting, showing, or selling the skulls and skeletons of other vertebrates? What do you think?

BONE BASICS

It also helped a lot when, in 1895, German scientist Wilhelm Roentgen (1845–1923) was experimenting with electricity and gases. He noticed that when he was working in a dark room, some images showed up on a special screen that was across the room. He did more tests and took the first X-ray picture of his wife's hand!

> **X-ray:** a powerful wave of energy that lets doctors see bones inside bodies.
>
> **WORDS TO KNOW**

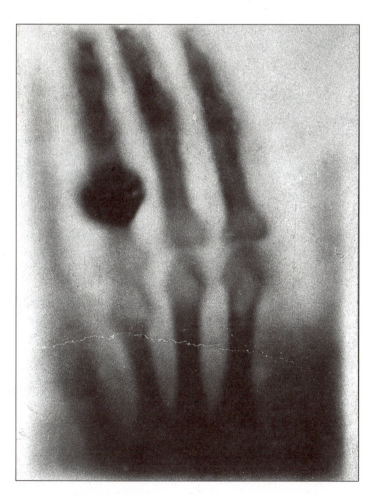

THE FIRST X-RAY IMAGE, 1895. CAN YOU SPOT THE RING?
CREDIT: WELLCOME IMAGES (CC BY 4.0)

The invention of the X-ray meant doctors did not need to open a body to see the bones inside. Now, scientists study bones all the time!

We are discovering more and more about how bones work and what they do for bodies. In the next chapter, we'll start with the bones in the head and neck!

> **? CONSIDER AND DISCUSS**
>
> **It's time to consider and discuss:** What would your body be like without bones?

PROJECT!

BONE HARD!

When bone cells are new, the tissue they create is very thin. It has lots of tiny holes in it. But these cells take calcium and other minerals from your blood. They clump the minerals together to make your bone tissue hard and strong. Model how tissue can get hard by adding salt to paper you have around your house.

> **SUPPLIES**
> * science journal and pencil
> * 2 large paper towels or 1 large sheet of tissue paper
> * ruler
> * scissors
> * tablespoon
> * salt (table salt is okay, but Epsom salt works better)
> * plastic microwavable cup
> * hot water
> * tweezers
> * plate

1 Start a scientific method worksheet in your science journal. Write this question at the top: "How do bones get hard?" Follow steps 2 and 3 of the scientific process on page 6 before starting the next step.

2 Look carefully at the paper towel or tissue. Hold it up to the light. Can you can see light coming through it? Record your observations in your journal.

3 Use the ruler and pencil to mark the paper towel or tissue paper into squares that are 1½ inches on each side. You want 40 squares total. Cut out the squares. Put them into two stacks of 20 squares each.

4 Pour 1 tablespoon of salt into the cup. Add 3 tablespoons of hot tap water and stir. Ask an adult to help you heat this in the microwave for about 20 seconds on high.

5 Stir again. If all the salt has **dissolved**, add another tablespoon of salt and stir.

WORDS TO KNOW

dissolve: when a solid becomes an invisible part of a liquid.

PROJECT!

6 Put one stack of 20 squares into the cup. Let the squares stay in the cup until they are completely soaked.

7 Take the soaked squares out of the cup. Carefully pull them apart. Use the tweezers to help you. Place each square in its own space on the plate. Let the squares dry.

> **DID YOU KNOW?**
> If hard-shelled turtles don't get enough calcium, their bones and shells can get so soft that they can be easily squished!

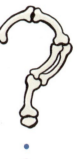

8 Feel a square that was not soaked. Feel a square that was soaked and then dried. What is the same? What is different? Write your observations in your journal.

9 Place all 20 squares of each kind in its own stack. When pressed together very hard, the stack of 20 salted squares is about the same thickness as some of the bones in your skull. Feel the weight of each stack. Try to bend them. What's different? Record your observations in your journal.

TRY THIS! Calcium is one of the most common minerals found on Earth. Your bone cells get the calcium they need from the food you eat. Go on a calcium search in your kitchen. Look at the nutrition labels for the word *calcium*. A good place to start is by looking at milk, cheese, yogurt, and ice cream!

PROJECT!

ELASTIC GIRL!

Have you seen *The Incredibles* movies? Mrs. Incredible can stretch, shrink, and bend in amazing ways, but never break. Although that is impossible in a live person or animal, you can imitate this with bones.

SUPPLIES
* science journal and pencil
* clean cooked chicken bones—it's best if you have pairs of the same kind
* plastic cup or bowl with a lid
* vinegar, soda, or lemon juice
* water
* towel

1 Examine the chicken bones you have gathered. Sketch the bones in your journal. Pay close attention to the surfaces and ends of the bones.

2 Very gently, try to bend each chicken bone without breaking it. Record your observations.

3 Place one bone from each pair in the plastic cup. Pour enough vinegar, soda, or lemon juice in the cup to cover the bones. Place the lid on the cup and put it in a place where no one will bother it for three days. What do you think will happen to the bones? Record your predictions in your journal.

4 After three days, remove the bones from the cups. Wash them off with plain water.

5 Record how each bone feels in your journal. Does it look the same? Try to bend each one. What do you notice? How do the soaked bones look and feel compared to the bones that stayed dry?

PROJECT!

6 Try to break each bone in a pair. Is one type easier to break? Look at the broken edges. Are they the same or different? Look inside each broken bone. What do you notice?

WHAT'S HAPPENING? Vinegar, soda, and lemon juice are all **acids**. The acids dissolve the calcium in the bones. When the calcium is gone, the bones are not as stiff. What might this mean for the bones inside your body?

> **TRY THIS!** Choose a different acid and repeat the project. If you used vinegar the first time, try using soda. Compare your results. What acid is most effective for dissolving calcium?

DYNAMIC DUO

For strong, healthy bones, your body needs both calcium and vitamin D. Vitamin D helps your body take in the calcium from the foods you eat. You can get vitamin D by drinking milk; eating egg yolks, fatty fish, and mushrooms; or just playing outside in the sun for 15 minutes every day! If you don't get both calcium and vitamin D, you might develop rickets. Rickets is a condition of having soft, weak bones that easily curve in or out.

WORDS TO KNOW

acid: a sour-tasting liquid that dissolves some minerals.

PROJECT!

EDIBLE BONES

Many animals eat the bones of other animals. Instead of eating real bones, follow this recipe to make yummy bone models for a snack.

IMPORTANT: Have an adult help with the baking!

SUPPLIES
* baking sheet
* cooking spray
* pizza dough
* rolling pin
* spoon
* tomato sauce
* shredded cheese
* hot pad
* plate

1 Turn the oven on to 400 degrees Fahrenheit and spray the baking sheet with cooking spray.

2 Place the pizza dough on a table or counter. Use the rolling pin to roll out the dough. This is your bone tissue.

3 Use the knife to cut out rectangles about 4 inches long by 3 inches wide.

DID YOU KNOW?

Wild animals often get calcium by chewing on bones. Cows, pigs, and our pets often get their calcium from crushed up bones, called bone meal, that is added to their food.

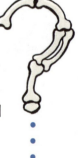

4 Spread some tomato sauce in the middle of each rectangle to make bone marrow. Sprinkle some cheese (which has the mineral calcium in it!) on the sauce.

5 Roll each rectangle into a long tube. Pinch the openings together to seal. Shape the ends to look like the ends of bones.

PROJECT!

6 Put each bone on the baking sheet. Bake for about 15 minutes. When the bones are golden brown, have an adult remove the pan from the oven.

7 Put the bones on a plate and let them cool for about 5 minutes before trying one!

> **TRY THIS!** Cut some of the dough into several diamond-shaped pieces. Imagine these are the flat bones in your skull. Put them very close together on the baking sheet. Sketch what you see in your journal. Check on them every 5 minutes as they bake. Watch as they fuse together, just like your skull bones do!

FINDING WILD BONES

Someday, you might find the skull or part of the skeleton of a wild animal. What should you do? The first thing is to look up the wild animal **salvage** laws in your state. Some skulls and skeletons you can **harvest**, but others you must leave alone. If it is legal to harvest it, make sure you get permission from your parents. Always wear gloves when picking up parts of a dead animal. Put the parts in a bucket. At home, fill with water and add a squirt of dish soap to the bucket. Put the bucket outside and leave it alone for several days. When the bones look clean, put on rubber gloves and take them out. Rinse them off and gently scrub them with an old toothbrush. Then, go to a nature center or museum in your area for help identifying your wild find!

> **WORDS TO KNOW**
>
> **salvage:** to pick up and save something that would otherwise be destroyed.
>
> **harvest:** to pick or gather something.

PROJECT!

EASY X-RAY

SUPPLIES
* thin cardboard
* pencil
* scissors
* shoebox lid
* glue
* screen
* sand

It is easy to see bones after an animal has died and all the skin and muscles are gone. But how can doctors see bones inside an animal that is still alive? One way is by using an X-ray machine. An X-ray machine sends out tiny beams of light. If the beams of light hit photographic film, the film turns black. If the beams of light get stopped by something, such as a hard bone, the film looks white.

1 Draw a bone on the piece of cardboard. Cut it out.

2 Cover the inside of the shoebox lid with glue. This will be your photographic film.

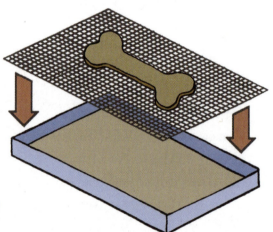

3 Put the screen on top of the lid edges. Put the cardboard bone on top of the screen.

4 Imagine the grains of sand are tiny light beams. Sprinkle sand over the entire area. Let the X-ray dry for 2 minutes before continuing.

5 Carefully pick up your screen and move it off to one side. Look at the inside of the shoebox lid. Is there a clear outline of the bone? Record your observations in your journal.

PROJECT!

TRY THIS! Make another cardboard bone or two. Imagine one is broken by cutting it in the wrong place. Put all the pieces on the screen before sprinkling sand. Does your X-ray image look different?

AFTER X-RAYS

X-rays are wonderful, but some scientists wanted to do even better. In 1972, two different scientists figured out how to do X-rays all the way around and through the body. These are called CT (or CAT) scans. And in 1977, another scientist discovered how to use magnetic fields, electric fields, and radio waves to take images of the inside of a body. These are called MRIs. What do you think could be next?

PHOTO CREDIT: ANNA BLOBAUM

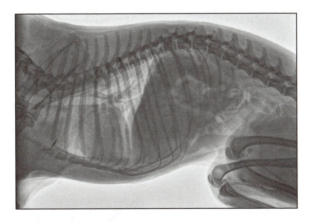

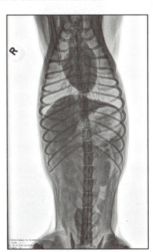

25

CHAPTER 2

HEAD AND NECK ABOVE THE REST

Sometimes, when people want you to think, they say, "Use your head!" That's because your brain is the organ that does the thinking for you. And that brain is housed in your head—inside your skull!

A skull has several jobs. One is to protect a brain from getting bruised or squished. Another job is to hold eyes, ears, nose, and teeth in the right places. Skulls also have muscles attached to them. These muscles let an animal open and close its mouth, wiggle its nose, swallow, make sounds, and hear.

WORDS TO KNOW

organ: a part of the body, such as the heart or lungs, that performs a certain function inside the body.

HEAD AND NECK ABOVE THE REST

> **? INVESTIGATE!**
>
> Why do some vertebrates have parts on their heads that humans don't have?

A skull is not just one big bone with holes in it. Most mammals have 35 or fewer bones in their skulls. Humans have 28.

Amphibians and reptiles have between 50 and 95. Some fish have 180 bones in their skulls—but birds have only five!

A HUMAN SKULL
CREDIT: SKELETONS: MUSEUM OF OSTEOLOGY IN OKLAHOMA CITY, OKLAHOMA

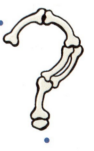

· · DID YOU KNOW? · ·

Invertebrates such as sponges, flatworms, and sea cucumbers don't have heads! If these animals are cut into pieces, each piece can grow into a whole new animal.

The size, shape, and the way a skull is put together can tell you a lot about the animal it came from. In fact, looking at the skull on a newly found skeleton is often the easiest way to identify the animal.

Let's take a closer look at the different parts of a skull.

SKULLS AND SKELETONS!

> **nostrils:** the one or two holes in a skull that bring air in and out and smells into the body.
>
> **keratin:** a protein that forms fingernails, beaks, hair, feathers, and claws.
>
> **WORDS TO KNOW**

THE NOSE KNOWS

Let's start at the nose. Gently pinch and wiggle the tip of your nose near your **nostrils**. Most of the human nose is made of cartilage, the same as the long, movable noses on elephants and tapirs.

Use your fingers to gently pinch the top of your nose, near your eyes. Here the nose bone is much stiffer. Can you move your nose there?

Animals in the dog, deer, and anteater families have long, bony snouts. Birds have nostrils on their beaks, which are made of **keratin**, not bone. Whale and dolphin nostrils can be found on top of their heads!

  Look at three-dimensional (3-D) bird skulls at this website! What can you learn from 3-D images that you might not be able to from 2-D images?

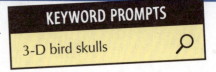

KEYWORD PROMPTS
3-D bird skulls 🔍

HEAD AND NECK ABOVE THE REST

JAWS

> **mandible:** the lower jaw bone.
>
> **WORDS TO KNOW**

Right under the noses of most animals are the jaws. The jaw bones are the ones that hold the teeth in those vertebrates that have teeth. The upper jaw is part of the skull. The lower jaw is called the mandible. It is attached to the skull with very strong muscles.

The jaws on sharks, snakes, frogs, and hippopotami can open very wide! The mandible of a cow is curved like the bottom of a rocking chair. What other jaw bones can you picture?

In most vertebrates, only the lower jaw can move. This is not true of birds. Both their top and bottom jaw bones, which are covered with beaks, can move. Have you ever seen a flamingo? The jaws of a flamingo are arched like a rainbow. What do you think this might mean for the flamingo's way of eating?

TOOTH TRUTH

Even though they grow out of your jaw bones, teeth are not bones! They are harder than bones. They don't have muscles attached to them and they don't make blood. Teeth cannot heal if they are broken, but they can fall out! For animals with teeth, the size, number, and placement of teeth can help identify the animal.

SKULLS AND SKELETONS!

> **predator:** an animal that hunts and eats other animals.
>
> **prey:** an animal that gets hunted and eaten by another animal.
>
> **species:** a group of animals that is different in some way from all other groups of animals.
>
> **cranium:** the part of the skull that encloses the brain.
>
> ### WORDS TO KNOW

THE EYES HAVE IT

What's above the nose on your face? Eyes! The eye holes in a skull, called eye sockets, give important clues about how well an animal sees and what it likes to eat.

For example, lions, wolves, and other **predators** usually have big eye holes that point forward. They are on the watch for their **prey**. Animals that eat plants and serve as prey for predators have big eye holes that point to the sides. They are watching out for danger!

Alligators, crocodiles, caiman, gavials, and some **species** of fish, including sole, flounder, and halibut, have eyes on top of their skulls. Birds and many fish and reptiles have bony eye rings. These rings help protect the eyes and keep them in the right shape.

Moles, shrews, and other animals that live mostly underground have tiny eyes with fewer bones protecting them. Why do you think this is?

CRANIUM CONNECTION

Above and behind the eye holes is the **cranium**, which covers the brain. Human craniums are big, smooth, eight-boned parts of the skull.

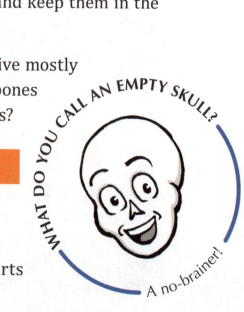

WHAT DO YOU CALL AN EMPTY SKULL? A no-brainer!

HEAD AND NECK ABOVE THE REST

Human craniums are different from the craniums of many other animals. Koalas have very small craniums made of 12 bones. Alligators have flat craniums made of many bones.

Gorillas, coyotes, mountain lions, and opossums have tall, bony crests in the middle of their craniums. The crest is a place to which large biting muscles can attach. Animals that have a crest usually have very strong bites or do a lot of chewing.

Antelope, bison, and some cows and goats have horns on their craniums. Deer, moose, and elk have antlers.

crest: a tuft or ridge on top of a head or hill.

horn: on the heads of some animals, a permanent point with a bony core covered with keratin.

antler: on the heads of some animals in the deer family, a bony point that is shed.

WORDS TO KNOW

THIS SKULL OF AN AFRICAN BUFFALO HAS HORNS.

SKULLS AND SKELETONS!

WORDS TO KNOW

dominance: being the leader because of greater strength.

vertebrae: the small bones that form the backbone.

palate: the roof of the mouth.

Both horns and antlers are used for protection. Male animals sometimes use their horns or antlers to see which one is the strongest—they are fighting for dominance.

THE NECK

Let's continue on our tour! The skull is attached to the rest of the body at the back of the cranium. This is where your vertebrae start. Reach around and feel the bumps on your neck—those are your vertebrae! Most vertebrates (except fish and frogs) have necks.

FLIP IT!

If a human cranium is turned upside down, you can see the parts that are usually hidden. Near the side between the back of the cranium and the eye, you'll spot bone bubbles. These protect the inner ear. In the middle of the upper jaw is the hard palate. This bone separates your nose and mouth areas. How far back the palate stretches in a skull is a clue to the type of animal skull.

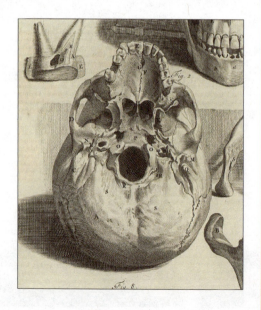

HEAD AND NECK ABOVE THE REST

Most mammals, including giraffes, whales, mice, and dogs, have seven vertebrae in their necks. Birds, such as swans, can have up to 25 neck vertebrae, while snakes have only two. Turtles have eight.

Feel the front of your neck, just under your mandible and above your voice box. This is where you would find your tongue bone, called the hyoid. Woodpeckers have long, flexible hyoid bones that wrap around their craniums—that makes a strong tongue!

DID YOU KNOW?
- Manatees, also called sea cows, have six neck vertebrae. Sloths have eight or nine.

The hyoid bones in lions and tigers are soft, which lets them roar. In house cats, the hyoid bones are hard, so they purr instead.

Now that we know about the bones on the very top floor, let's travel down the stairs of the spine to find out about bones in the torso in the next chapter!

CONSIDER AND DISCUSS

It's time to consider and discuss: Why do some vertebrates have parts on their heads that humans don't have?

  See how well you can match pictures of animal skulls and their names! **Play a matching game at this website.**

KEYWORD PROMPTS
Sporcle skulls match

PROJECT!

PERFECT PROTECTION

One of the most important jobs of your skull is to protect your brain. Imagine if all you had was your skin covering your brain. Danger! Can you design a skull to protect it?

SUPPLIES
- science journal and pencil
- 10 to 20 water balloons
- water
- bucket
- measuring tape
- plastic food tub with lid, large enough to hold filled water balloon
- bubble wrap, paper towels, cloth rags, or other padding material
- tape
- chair

1 Fill the balloons with water and tie them shut. Place them in the bucket. These are your skin-covered skulls.

2 Predict how far you can drop a filled balloon without it breaking. Record your prediction in your journal.

3 Put a balloon in one hand. Stretch your arm out straight. Use the measuring tape to make sure the balloon is 1 foot above the ground. Turn your hand over and drop the balloon—don't throw it! Record the results.

4 Repeat the test, moving your hand higher or lower until you find the lowest height at which the balloon breaks. This is the **breaking point**.

5 Sketch some skull designs in your science journal. How can you protect your balloon brain?

WHAT DO YOU CALL A SKELETON THAT PLAYED IN THE SNOW ALL DAY?

A numbskull!

WORDS TO KNOW

breaking point: the place at which something can no longer stay together.

PROJECT!

ALWAYS WEAR A SPORTS HELMET TO PROTECT YOUR BRAIN!

6 Use the plastic container and padding materials to make a skull for a balloon. Tape the container shut. Test it at the breaking point. Does the balloon break?

7 Repeat the test, moving your hand higher or lower until you find the new breaking point, or the lowest height, at which the balloon breaks. Use a chair to get the balloon even higher. Can you adjust your design to be a better protector?

TRY THIS! Find an old helmet that no one needs to use anymore. How well does it perform in the drop test? Note that you cannot use the helmet for head protection after doing this project!

PROJECT!
HOW BIG IS THE BRAIN?

Animals can be almost the same length and weight but have very different sized brains. An opossum and house cat can be about the same size. But an opossum has a much smaller brain. One simple measurement scientists can make and compare is the volume of an animal's skull. The brain volume will not say which animal is smarter, but it does provide another way to identify an animal.

SUPPLIES
* science journal and pencil
* 4 shoes of different sizes and styles
* newspaper
* rice, unpopped popcorn kernels, birdseed, or sand to use as fill
* measuring cups and spoons
* box or bag

IMPORTANT: Do not eat any of the materials used in this project.

1 Which shoe do you think will hold the greatest volume of fill? Start a scientific method worksheet and write your hypothesis in your journal.

2 Put one shoe on the newspaper. Pour in the fill until the shoe can hold no more. Hold the filled shoe over the box or bag so you don't make too much of a mess. Pour the fill out of the shoe into the measuring cups. Record the data in your journal.

3 Repeat for each of the shoes. Be sure to record the data in your journal! Was your prediction correct?

THINK ABOUT IT! Does the volume a shoe holds tell you everything about the shoe? What does it tell you? What might it tell you about an animal's brain?

WORDS TO KNOW

volume: the amount of space an object takes up.

PROJECT!
ROCK FACE

Scientists often use the bones they find to solve mysteries. What animals lived here? What did they look like? What did they eat?

> **SUPPLIES**
> * rock that fits in the palm of your hand
> * water
> * soap
> * clay
> * yarn or string
> * scissors
> * toothpick
> * paint

1 Wash the rock with soap and water and let it dry. Imagine the rock is an animal skull. Turn it around in your hands. Which part is the cranium? Which part is the nose? Can you see a face in it? Remember, the lower jaw on most animals is not attached to the skull.

2 Mold the clay around the rock to form a nose, ears, eye sockets, and eyebrows. For hair, cut the string into small pieces. Use the toothpick to poke one end of a string piece into the clay.

3 Let the clay dry. Paint the face to make it look more alive. Can you remember what the rock looked like underneath? How is this similar to a skull under a face?

TRY THIS! Collect some bones, such as chicken, turkey, pork, beef, and fish, from a meal you have eaten. Have an adult help you to boil the bones and wash them to make sure they are clean. Imagine they are part of the body for the rock skull you made. Can you draw a skeleton to go with it? Can you draw the body with skin on it?

Check this out! See how a human skull was made into a face!

KEYWORD PROMPTS
forensic facial reconstruction

PROJECT!

VISION TEST

Human eyes are in front of the skull. How does this affect how you see? Bring your hands together with your palms and fingers touching. Put your thumbs on your nose. Look at a sign, door, or tree, far away. Do you even notice your hands? Try to read a sign or book. You can probably still see everything pretty clearly. You get clues from both eyes and your brain puts the information together.

While facing a computer or sign, open your hands so the palms face you until you can no longer see the sign. This is what vision is like for animals with eyes on the sides of their heads. However, they can see farther on the sides. Get permission to sit in the driver's seat of a car. Look to each side for the side-view mirrors. These mimic the way an animal with eyes on the side can see behind itself. Humans have invented ways to have eyes of both kinds!

SUPPLIES
* science journal and pencil
* table or desk and chair
* clay
* metal washer
* ruler
* sharpened pencil

1 Make a chart like this in your journal.

Distance from edge	Right eye open	Left eye open	Both eyes open

WORDS TO KNOW

vision: the ability to see things using your eyes.

PROJECT!

2 Sit at a table or desk. Put your arms down in front of you with your elbows at the edge of the table, your hands on the table, and your fingers together. Place a small piece of clay on the table where your fingers come together.

3 Stand the metal washer in the clay so an edge is facing you. Measure the distance from the edge of the table to the washer. Record this number in your journal.

4 Cover one eye with one hand. Pick up the sharpened pencil with the opposite hand. Try to poke the pencil point through the washer hole without leaning closer. Record how many tries it takes in your journal.

5 Repeat the experiment closing your other eye. Repeat the experiment with both eyes open. Try it with the pencil in each hand.

6 Move the washer and clay farther away. Record the distance and repeat the experiment. Move the washer and clay closer and try everything again! What are your results?

> **THINK ABOUT IT!** Did you do better with one eye than the other? Why do you think this is the case? Just for fun, try playing one-eyed catch with a soft ball.

PROJECT!

LOOK AROUND!

Owls and tarsiers are animals with great big eyes. Their eyes have bones that hold them in place so the eyes cannot move to look up, down, or side-to-side. The only way these animals can look around is to use their necks! Test your neck to see how it helps you look around.

SUPPLIES
- ✳ science journal and pencil
- ✳ 5 pieces copy paper
- ✳ markers
- ✳ chair with shoulder-high back
- ✳ measuring tape
- ✳ pencil
- ✳ tape

1 Use the paper and markers to make posters, each with a line of random letters and numbers.

2 Put the chair in the middle of the room. Use the measuring tape to make a straight line from each side of the chair out to a wall or another chair. Tape one poster to the wall (or another chair) at sitting eye level on each side, at least 6 feet away.

3 Use the measuring tape to make a straight line from directly behind the chair. Tape one poster to the wall (or another chair) at sitting eye level here, at least 6 feet away.

4 Use the measuring tape to make a straight line at an angle from the chair to each side between the other posters. Tape one poster to the wall (or another chair) at sitting eye level to each side, at least 6 feet away.

• DID YOU KNOW? •

It is not true that an owl (or any other vertebrate) can turn its head all the way around. If it did, it would pinch the spinal nerve and the animal would become paralyzed!

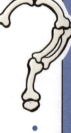

PROJECT!

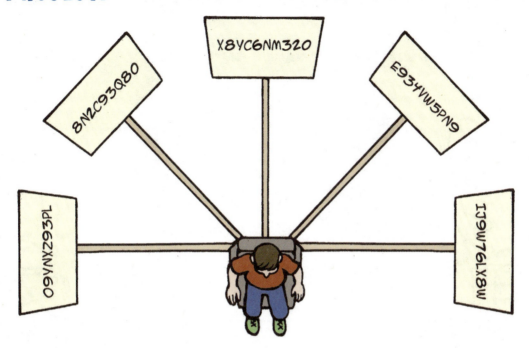

5 Sit in the chair. Press both of your shoulders back so they touch the chair. Turn your neck to the right as far as you can. Both shoulders should still touch the chair back. Read and record the letters and numbers on the poster.

6 Turn your neck to the left as far as you can. Read and record the letters and numbers on the poster. If you were an owl or sloth, you would be able to turn your neck so far to the right, you could see the poster lined up with your left shoulder! That is 270 degrees! What about the poster behind the chair? Is there any way for a creature to see all the way behind them?

TRY THIS! Use a **protractor** to figure out how many degrees your neck can turn.

WORDS TO KNOW

paralyzed: unable to move.

protractor: a device for drawing and measuring angles.

41

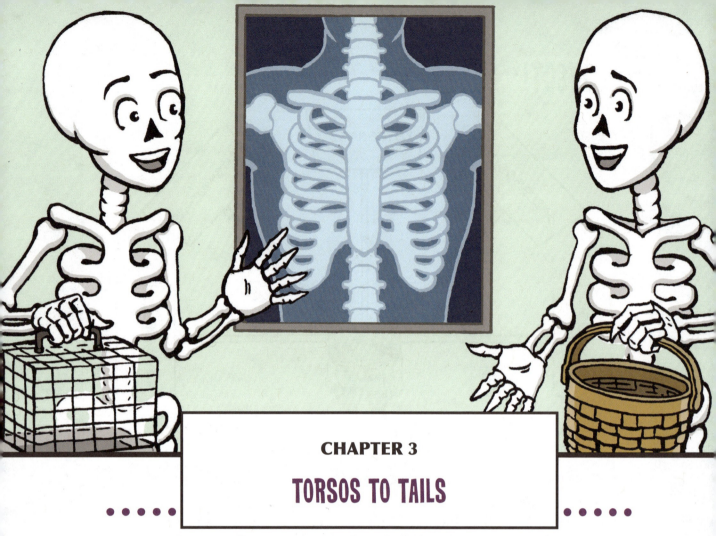

CHAPTER 3
TORSOS TO TAILS

The area between your head and your legs is pretty important. After all, this is where most of your critical organs are! You need to have some good bones to protect these organs so you can bound through life without worrying too much about hurting them.

This middle part of your body is called the torso. It holds important parts of all 11 of the vertebrate organ systems, including the heart, lungs, and stomach. It is the job of your skeleton to provide support and protection so your systems can keep working.

? INVESTIGATE!

How does having an upright body change a skeleton?

TORSOS TO TAILS

The bones of your torso include your collarbones and shoulder blades, ribs and sternum, vertebrae, and pelvis. The torso also provides the connection points for the head, arms, and legs.

To do their job, parts of the torso skeleton act like a cage. Other parts of the torso skeleton act more like a basket. Different vertebrates have some very different torsos. Let's take a look!

> **organ system:** a group of tissues in a living body that work together to do a specific job.
>
> **sternum:** the flat bone that connects the top ribs in some vertebrates.
>
> **pelvis:** the large bony structure near the end of a vertebrate's backbone where the hind limbs attach.
>
> ### WORDS TO KNOW

SHRUG IT OFF

The top part of the torso is most like a cage. Near the head on the front side of humans, frogs, lizards, and mammals that climb, fly, or hold things with their front feet are thin collarbones. These connect with big, flat shoulder blades in the back and serve as a place for arms to attach.

In birds, the collarbones are joined and make the wishbone. Have you ever wished on a wishbone? Many other vertebrates have no collarbones at all!

WHAT DOES A SKELETON EAT AT A RESTAURANT?

Spare ribs!

SKULLS AND SKELETONS!

> **rib cage:** the bony box in the chest of vertebrates that is made mostly of ribs. It protects the heart and lungs.
>
> **keel:** a bony ridge on the center line of a bird's sternum.
>
> **WORDS TO KNOW**

Right below the collarbones are the ribs. The rib bones connect to the vertebrae in the back. In humans, the top seven pairs of ribs are joined together in the front at the sternum. The 12 pairs of ribs in humans are called the **rib cage**. The ribs protect the heart and lungs.

Snakes have very long torsos with up to 400 ribs that go all the way to their tails. And frogs have no ribs at all!

Horses, lions, bison, and elephants have heavy heads and powerful front legs. The backs of their vertebrae that connect to the ribs look like they have long bony handles sticking out. Strong muscles are attached here to help these animals hold their heads up and move their forelegs.

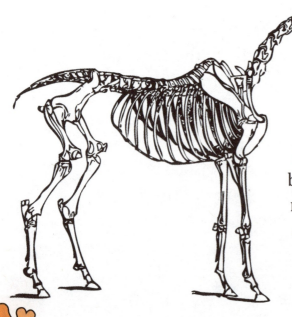

Most birds don't have heavy heads or powerful front legs, but they do have wings. Their chest muscles connect to the **keel**, which is a ridge in the front of the sternum. Hollow bones keep birds light to help them fly.

TORSOS TO TAILS

• DID YOU KNOW? •
Penguins, emus, ostriches, rheas, and kiwis are birds that can't fly. They do not have keels on their sternums!

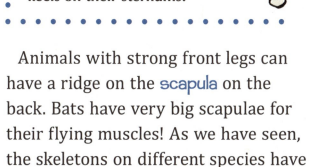

> **scapula:** a shoulder blade.
>
> **adapt:** to make changes to better survive in an environment.
>
> **adaptation:** something about a plant or animal that helps it survive.
>
> **fossil:** the remains of any organism, including animals and plants, that have been preserved in rock.
>
> **evaporate:** to convert from a liquid to a gas.
>
> **WORDS TO KNOW**

Animals with strong front legs can have a ridge on the scapula on the back. Bats have very big scapulae for their flying muscles! As we have seen, the skeletons on different species have adapted to fit their needs. What other adaptations can you think of?

LOWER FLOOR

On many vertebrates, a section of the skeleton below the ribs is just vertebrae, with no other bones. This bone structure makes it possible for you to twist your body from side to side, curl up in a ball, do a back bend, and do the twist!

FOSSILIZED!

If a buried bone is left alone, sometimes it can become a fossil. One type of fossil is made when water filled with minerals soaks into the holes in the bone. When the water evaporates, the minerals are left behind. After a very long time has passed, the holes become filled with minerals. This preserves the much harder bone as a fossil. This is a lot like what happened in the project "Bone Hard!" in Chapter 1!

SKULLS AND SKELETONS!

> **upright:** sitting or standing with the back in a vertical line.
> **vertical:** straight up and down.
>
> **WORDS TO KNOW**

Your backbone can move in a lot of ways, but it does have its limits.

The pelvis is located just before the tail end of the torso. This is where the hind limbs are attached on those vertebrates that have them. The hip joint has a ball-and-socket joint, which lets the top of the hind leg move in many directions. Take a look at the illustration on page 14 to see a ball-and-socket joint.

Because humans stand on two legs, their pelvis acts like a wide, bony basket. It holds a lot of organs! Animals that walk on four legs have thinner pelvises. The pelvis on a bird is fused with its vertebrae to make a very stiff, unbending lower back. The pelvis on fish has turned into some fins!

REPTILE TORSOS

Different species have different torsos. Alligators and crocodiles have tiny bits of bone under the scales on their backs. Turtles take it even farther. Turtle shells are made of bone. The bone tissues that make the vertebrae, ribs, and pelvis all join together and grow outside a turtle's skin. If you look inside the shell of a dead turtle, you can see these bones.

TALE OF TAILS

You'll find tailbones at the very end of the line of vertebrae. In humans and great apes, four bones are fused together to make a very short, not very useful tailbone. Humans spend a lot of time *upright*, with their bodies in a *vertical* line. We stand on two legs or sit with our back upright. We do pretty well without a long tailbone.

TORSOS TO TAILS

> **horizontal:** straight across from side to side.
>
> **WORDS TO KNOW**

However, most other vertebrates spend most of their time with their torsos in a horizontal line. The head and skull make their bodies heavy at one end. A long tail at the back end can help an animal balance. Have you seen squirrels climbing and jumping in trees? They use their tails a lot!

Tails can help vertebrates in many other ways as well. Alligators, dolphins, and whales use their tails to swim. Kangaroos use their tails to push off when they jump and to hold them up when they rest. Spider monkeys, opossums, anteaters, and kinkajous have tails that can hold onto objects. Birds use their tails to steer their flight. Horses and cows use their tails to swat flies.

A SKELETON OF A RED SQUIRREL, 1924
CREDIT: PANDER, CHRISTIAN HEINRICH

Torsos are key for another reason—they provide a place for arms and legs to connect to the body. We'll learn more about those in the next chapter!

> **? CONSIDER AND DISCUSS**
>
> **It's time to consider and discuss:** How does having an upright body change a skeleton?

PROJECT!

SPOOL SPINE

Your vertebrae are important bones in many ways. They protect your spinal cord and offer places for many other bones and muscles to attach. You tested your neck vertebrae in Chapter 2. Now make a model of how it works.

SUPPLIES
- science journal and pencil
- 3 thread spools of different sizes
- marker
- pencil
- craft foam
- scissors
- hole punch
- straw or tubing that can fit through the middle hole of the three stacked spools
- water
- dropper

When you were a baby, you had 33 separate vertebrae. As you grew older, five vertebrae in your hip area fused together to make the sacrum. Four fused together to make the tailbone. Right now, you have 24 individual vertebrae and nine fused together in two different groups. The individual vertebrae are in three groups: seven neck vertebrae, 12 chest vertebrae, and five lower back ones. They are hard, they come in several sizes, they are a little wider at the top and bottom, and they have a hole in the middle.

1 Use the marker to write "7 neck" on the side of the smallest spool. Label the biggest spool "12 chest." Label the medium spool "5 lower back."

WORDS TO KNOW

sacrum: a triangular bone in the lower back that is located between the two hipbones of the pelvis.

PROJECT!

2 Rub the ends of two of the spools together for one minute. When you stop, immediately touch the rubbed ends. They should feel warm. That is what would happen if you were really stretching or moving around a lot. It would not be good if our bones rubbed against each other like that. Luckily, a thin disk separates the vertebrae.

3 Use the pencil to trace one end of each spool on the craft foam. Cut out the foam and punch a hole through the center using the hole punch or your pencil.

4 Stack your spools, alternating them with craft foam, on your straw, going medium, large, small, with the medium spool at the bottom. The straw is the spinal cord that goes through the middle of your vertebrae. The spinal cord is the information highway that connects your brain to the rest of your body. Small nerve fibers go out from the spinal cord, between the vertebrae, and to the muscles in your body.

5 Test your spool spine. How far can it move from side to side? How many vertebrae do you estimate you would need to allow it to bend enough to make an L shape?

6 Drip water through the straw. What happens if your spine is bent? What happens if your spine gets pinched shut? This can happen in real life. If you can't straighten out the spinal cord and restore the information flow, you might lose the ability to move.

> **TRY THIS!** String tri-beads, or beads with three bumps, to make a mock spine. How many vertebrae do you need to curl up in a ball?

PROJECT!

BONE BUILDING

Bones and muscles work together. If you use a muscle a lot, it gets bigger and stronger. It also pulls more on the attached bones. The bone reacts by becoming thicker and stronger, too. Many people put most of their effort into getting big arm muscles. But some of the most important muscles to keep strong and healthy are the core muscles in your torso. If you do these exercises three or four times a week, your torso bones and muscles will get bigger and stronger!

1 Lay on your back. Bend your knees so that your feet are under them. Push your bottom up off the floor to make a bridge. Keep your head and shoulders on the ground. Count to 10, then slowly move your bottom down. Repeat this five times.

2 Lay on your belly with your arms stretched out in front of your head. Lift your arms and legs off the ground so that you look like a superhero flying through the air. Count to 10, then slowly lower your arms and legs. Repeat this five times.

3 Lay on your belly with the palms of your hands near your shoulders. Push up with your arms and feet so that your body makes a curved line from your head to your toes. Count to 10, then slowly lower your body to the ground. Repeat this five times.

TRY THIS! Put a stuffed animal or small ball between your knees during each exercise. How does this change how your body moves?

DID YOU KNOW?
Professional archers and baseball and softball players use one arm a lot more than the other. Their bodies react by making the muscles and bones in their dominant arms much bigger and stronger. Sometimes, they joke that they look like fiddler crabs!

PROJECT!

PUTTING IT ALL TOGETHER!

SUPPLIES
* 10 to 12 craft sticks
* masking tape
* animal stencils (optional)
* crayons or markers

Most found skeletons are missing some pieces. Putting them together is like doing a puzzle, without a picture to help! In 1869, a drawing Edward Drinker Cope (1840–1897) made of an ancient, swimming reptile fossil skeleton he found was put in a book. But he had made a mistake. He had drawn the skull at the end of the tail instead of at the end of the neck! You would never make that mistake . . . or would you?

1 Lay the craft sticks side by side to make a board. Place a piece of tape over the middle.

2 Flip the board over. Use animal stencils or simply free draw a vertebrate animal on this side. Be sure to color it in.

3 Take the tape off. Remove any sticks that do not have any color on them. Drop the remaining sticks in a jumbled pile.

4 Try to put the skeleton back together. Did you succeed?

TRY THIS! Do this project with a friend and swap the skeletons. Or remove one or two sticks to **simulate** a real-life find!

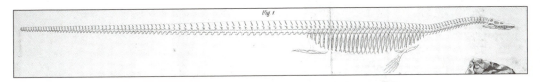

THIS SHOWS COPE'S MISTAKE—THE HEAD IS AT THE WRONG END OF THE SKELETON.

WORDS TO KNOW

simulate: to imitate certain conditions for the purpose of testing or study.

PROJECT!

BALANCING ACT

Animals' tails get used in many ways. Binturongs and some monkeys hold onto things with their tails. Beavers use their tails to pack mud on their dams. Peacocks use their tails to show off. Squirrels, mice, and other animals that climb and scamper use their tails for balance. Do some testing to see how tails affect balance!

> **SUPPLIES**
> * science journal and pencil
> * new pencil, with an eraser tip
> * marker
> * ruler
> * chenille stems (pipe cleaners)
> * scissors
> * clay (optional)

1 Balance the new pencil in a horizontal line on one finger. Use the marker to make a line where the **balance point** is.

2 Think of the eraser end as being the head. Use the ruler to measure the distance from the eraser end to the balance point. Record this number in your science journal.

3 Think of the tip end as being the tail. Wrap the end of one chenille stem around the tip end of the pencil. Balance it again. Use the marker to make a line where the new balance point is.

WORDS TO KNOW

balance point: the spot on a beam where the weight is equal on each side.

PROJECT!

4 Use the ruler to measure the distance from the eraser end to the new balance point. Record this number in your journal. Compare this to your first test. Is the new balance point closer to the eraser end or farther away?

5 Cut the chenille stem into two pieces of different sizes. Repeat the balancing test for each piece. Record your results in your journal. What did you learn?

> **TRY THIS!** Elephants have a huge head and a tiny tail. Peacocks have a small head and a huge tail. Do you get different results if you use a longer or shorter pencil? What if you use a small ball of clay to make a heavier head?

TRUE TAIL!

In December 2005, a fisherman in Florida found a young dolphin caught in a crab trap. Local animal doctors worked to save her life, but her tail had to be cut off. She was taken to an aquarium to heal and was given the name Winter. Later, the aquarium worked with a company that makes artificial arms and legs for people to get a new tail for Winter. Since this was the first time anyone had made a dolphin tail, they had to try many different designs. Winter also had to learn how to wear and use the tail. Now, she can easily swim with the other dolphins at the aquarium!

  See Winter the dolphin swimming with her new tail at this website.

KEYWORD PROMPTS
Winter dolphin cam

CHAPTER 4
OUT ON A LIMB

There is an amazing amount of variety when it comes to bodies. For example, snakes have no arms or legs, while humans have two arms and two legs, and dogs have four legs, but no arms!

Arms and legs are known as limbs. Limbs are parts of the skeleton that attach to the sides of the torso near the top and bottom. The limbs closest to the head are called forelimbs. Forelimbs help an animal move. Forelimbs on humans—your arms—are attached to the shoulder blades and collarbones.

Bats and birds have forelimbs called wings. Fish forelimbs are called fins. Whales, dolphins, sea turtles, and penguins have flippers as their forelimbs.

 INVESTIGATE!

Which are longer and stronger, your arms or your legs? How can you tell?

OUT ON A LIMB

• DID YOU KNOW? •

Snakes are vertebrates that don't have any limbs at all. Whales and dolphins have forelimbs, but not hind limbs.

limb: a part of a vertebrate's skeleton that is mostly used for movement.

forelimb: the arms, legs, wings, flippers, or fins on a vertebrate that are attached closest to the head.

hind limb: the legs that are attached closest to the tail end of a vertebrate.

WORDS TO KNOW

Limbs attached to the pelvis are hind limbs. Hind limbs are mostly used for jumping, swimming, running, or walking.

Animals that live in the water can have flippers or fins as hind limbs. Elephant seals have flippers as hind limbs. For most other animals, including humans, the hind limbs are simply called legs. Raccoons, chickens, and lizards all have legs.

KNOW YOUR KNEES!

Bend your leg. Which way does your knee point? Look at a picture of a dog, cat, cow, bird, or other vertebrate with hind limbs. Which way does its knees point? For a long time, people thought that only primates had knees that bent forward. But that was before people had really studied skeletons. The part of the hind limb that points backward on most vertebrates is actually the heel! The knee (where the femur bone meets the tibia and fibula bones) is up higher on most animals. When it is covered with muscles and fur, it looks like part of the torso instead of a limb.

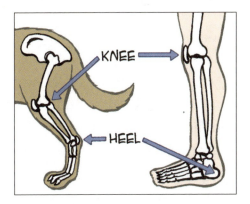

55

SKULLS AND SKELETONS!

> **humerus:** the arm bone between the shoulder and elbow.
>
> **ulna:** one of the thin bones between the humerus and wrist.
>
> **radius:** one of the thin bones between the humerus and wrist.
>
> **WORDS TO KNOW**

LOOKING AT LIMBS

Human arms and legs are very much alike. Each arm has one long, strong bone at the top. This bone, called the humerus, goes from the shoulder to the elbow. The ulna and radius are two thinner bones that go from the elbow to the wrist.

BROKEN BONES

What happens if you break a bone? Have you ever scraped your knee or gotten a cut? Blood fills the wound, gets thick and sticky, and makes a clot, which forms a scab. Then, the skin cells form new tissue. More blood brings in the minerals needed to form new skin. When the new skin is done, the scab falls away.

The same thing happens when you break a bone. Blood makes a clot around the broken parts. As more blood brings in bone-building minerals, a soft tissue forms over the ends. Just like when your body is first making bones, the holes in the tissue fill in with calcium and other hard minerals. A few weeks later, the bone is back together. Doctors often put a hard cast around a broken arm or leg or even put in a metal rod to hold the broken pieces in the right place. This is to make sure the broken edges are lined up before the body starts building new bone.

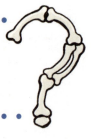

DID YOU KNOW?

Even animals that walk on four legs have only two knees.

OUT ON A LIMB

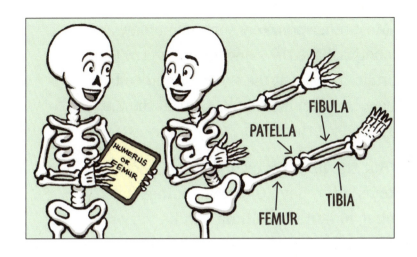

femur: the upper bone in a hind limb.

tibia: one of the thin bones between the femur and the ankle.

fibula: one of the thin bones between the femur and the ankle.

patella: the kneecap.

WORDS TO KNOW

Each leg also has one long, strong bone at the top. The femur goes from the hip to the knee. The tibia and fibula are two thinner bones that go from the knee to the ankle. The knee joint has a special bone called the patella. The patella protects the joint and is also where muscle tendons are attached.

SKELETONS OF BIG CATS
CREDIT: SKELETONS: MUSEUM OF OSTEOLOGY IN OKLAHOMA CITY, OKLAHOMA

SKULLS AND SKELETONS!

WORDS TO KNOW

primate: any member of the group of mammals that includes humans, monkeys, and apes.

lever: a bar that is used to lift a heavy load.

Most other primates, such as monkeys and baboons, have the same limb pattern. The forelimb starts at the shoulder and ends at the wrist. The hind limb starts at the hip and ends at the ankle.

But the limb pattern changes a lot in other animals! The bones often have the same names, but the size, shape, and number of bones in a limb can be very different. Animals as different as frogs and bison have limb bones that are fused. This makes the bones stronger.

Wolves, lions, flamingoes, and antelope have leg bones that in humans are part of the wrist, hand, ankle, and foot! Why do you think different species adapt in different ways?

DID YOU KNOW?

Your funny bone is not a bone! It is a nerve trapped between the bone and skin when the elbow is bent. If you bump your elbow hard, it can cause your hand to tingle.

LIMBS IN MOTION

You know you use your legs for walking and your arms for lifting, but how do they work? Limbs act as levers. Levers are simple tools that help move or lift things.

The size and strength of the limbs depend on the animal and how they use them. For example, hummingbirds have strong forelimbs—those are their wings. Because they don't use their hind limbs for much, hummingbird hind limbs are pretty weak.

OUT ON A LIMB

Geese have strong forelimbs and strong hind limbs. They use their wings for flying and their hind limbs for swimming. Frogs have legs that are longer than their bodies. This helps them to jump farther. Cheetahs have long legs that make it easier to run fast.

Instead of using their limbs to move, porpoises and other **aquatic** mammals use their bodies and tails. They have very short limbs they use mostly to steer themselves through the water.

aquatic: having to do with water.

rodent: the group of mammals that use their ever-growing front teeth to chew on things. Rodents make up more than half of all mammals on Earth and include mice, rats, squirrels, chipmunks, beavers, and gerbils.

dissect: to cut something apart to study what is inside.

WORDS TO KNOW

WHERE ARE THE BONES?

Wild animals live and die all around us. You might expect to see lots of bones and skeletons just lying around, but nature has a way of recycling things. Many **rodents** chew on bones. This helps them keep their teeth, which are always growing, from becoming too long. The bones also give them some minerals they need. Some predators will eat the bones of their prey. Snakes eat entire animals, bones and all. The acid in their stomach digests the bones. Owls eat entire animals as well. But they do not digest the bones. Inside their stomachs, the bones and fur get made into hard balls that get coughed out as owl pellets. People collect and clean these pellets. They **dissect** the clean pellets to find out what the owl ate for dinner!

You can dissect an owl pellet virtually at this website.

KEYWORD PROMPTS

virtual owl pellet dissection

SKULLS AND SKELETONS!

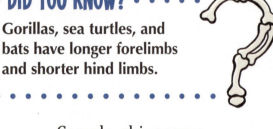

DID YOU KNOW?
Gorillas, sea turtles, and bats have longer forelimbs and shorter hind limbs.

Camels, rhinoceros, donkeys, chipmunks, and many other vertebrates spend most of their time on four legs. This gives the animals better balance. It also helps them run faster and be stronger.

Just as you can learn to walk on your hands, circus and show animals can be trained to walk on two legs. Some animals born without limbs do as well.

Now that we know more about limbs, in the next chapter let's look at what's dangling at the end of your arms and legs—hands and feet!

 CONSIDER AND DISCUSS

It's time to consider and discuss: Which are longer and stronger, your arms or your legs? How can you tell?

  Goats are very athletic four-legged creatures. When this goat was born without hind legs, he didn't let it stop him! **See for yourself at this website.**

KEYWORD PROMPTS
two-legged goat video

PROJECT!

MUSCLE MODEL

Bones give muscles a sturdy place to connect. Strong bones make it possible for strong muscles to do their work of moving body parts. In this experiment, twist ties and pencils will represent bones and rubber bands will represent muscles.

SUPPLIES
* science journal and pencil
* twist ties
* thin rubber bands
* small toy or other object
* pencils, pens, or craft sticks
* wide rubber bands

1 Place one twist tie around one loop end of a thin rubber band. Place the other loop end of the rubber band around a small toy you want to pick up.

2 Holding just one end of the twist tie, lift the item as high as you can. What happens? Record your observations in your science journal.

3 Repeat steps 1 and 2 using a thin rubber band and a pencil instead of a twist tie. Record what happens.

4 Repeat steps 1 and 2 using a wide rubber band and a pencil. Record what happens.

THINK ABOUT IT! What do you think would happen in your body if a strong muscle pulled on a thin bone? A thin muscle pulled on a strong bone? What could you add to your pencil to help keep the rubber band muscle in place? How can you test it?

PROJECT!

LIMBS AS LEVERS

Some of the bones in your skeleton act as levers. Try this test on your forelimbs, which have three different levers. After you are done, identify your other lever limbs and design your own test for them!

SUPPLIES
* table, desk, or back of wide chair
* soft ball
* measuring tape
* science journal and pencil

1 Lay one entire arm, from your armpit to your wrist, flat on a table or desk. Hang your wrist over the edge with your palm facing down.

2 Put a soft ball in your hand. Throw it as far as you can, without lifting your arm up!

3 Measure how far the ball went. Record this number in your journal.

4 Lay the same arm down in the same place, this time from armpit to elbow. Keep your forearm upright.

5 Place the ball in your hand. Throw it as far as you can, moving your elbow and wrist, but without lifting your arm up!

6 Measure how far the ball went. Record this number in your journal.

PROJECT!

7 Place the ball in your hand. Raise your arm straight up. Throw the ball as far as you can, moving your entire arm forward (but not backward).

8 Measure how far the ball went. Record this number in your journal.

9 Place the ball in your hand. This time, move your arm up and backward, before throwing the ball forward. What do you notice about the difference in distances? What does that show about the usefulness of levers?

WHEN DOES A SKELETON LAUGH? When something tickles its funny bone!

TRY THIS! Repeat this project using your other arm. Is there a difference? When is it most noticeable?

PROJECT!

SUPPLIES
* measuring tape
* science journal and pencil

MEASURING UP!

A skeleton likes to be balanced. It has a lot of parts that are similar in size, even if they are not close to each other. Do these simple comparisons to see how you measure up!

1 Place one end of the measuring tape where the top of your leg meets your hip. Stretch the other end down to your knee. Record this number in your journal as femur length.

2 Stretch the measuring tape between your fingertips as you open your arms as wide as you can. Record this number in your journal as your arm span.

3 Use the measuring tape to measure from your elbow to your wrist. Record this number in your journal as your forearm length.

PROJECT!

4 Get ready to compare! Add your femur length together four times. This number should be close to your arm span number. Both of these should be close to your height! Use the measuring tape to check!

5 Sit down and take off a shoe. Put your foot on a forearm, right between the elbow and the wrist. Does it fit?

> **TRY THIS!** Compare the length of your foot, your femur, and your lower leg. If you were a frog, these would all be about the same size!

A KING'S THUMB

A long time ago, there were no rulers, yard sticks, or measuring tapes. People often used their body parts to measure things. See how close your body measures to the old standards.

King Henry I of England (1068–1135) said a yard was the distance from his nose to the thumb of his outstretched arm. (Today, it is 36 inches.)

In ancient Egypt, a cubit was the distance from the elbow to the fingertips. (Today, it is about 18 inches.)

An inch was the width of a man's thumb.

A foot was the length of the average man's foot.

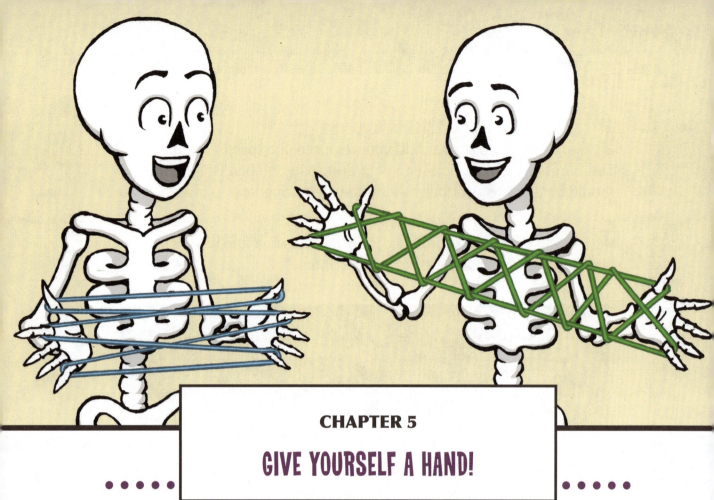

CHAPTER 5
GIVE YOURSELF A HAND!

If you are wearing shoes and socks, take them off so you can compare a hand and a foot. What do you notice about them? How are they different from each other? How are they similar?

Most humans have 27 bones in each hand and 26 bones in each foot. The hands and feet together contain more than half of the bones in a human body!

Bend your fingers and toes. Spread them apart. It might not always look like it, but most other animals have the same basic layout for the ends of their arms and legs. Depending on how the hands and feet are used, they might have more or fewer bones.

? INVESTIGATE!

How many ways do you use your hands and feet?

GIVE YOURSELF A HAND!

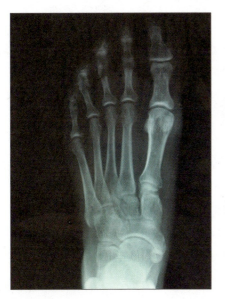

FOOT X-RAY

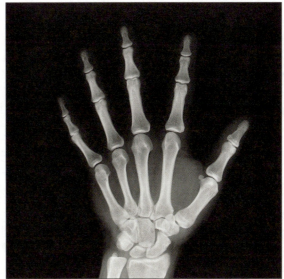

HAND X-RAY

WAVE YOUR HAND!

Hands are found at the end of the forelimbs. What do you use your hands for? Hands can grab or hold things. They can also help an animal move. Humans, apes, and monkeys all have similar hands that can do similar jobs, as do koalas, opossums, and pandas.

Each human hand has 13 wrist and palm bones. The thumb has two bones and each of the four fingers has three bones. Can you feel them with your other fingers?

  Many people dream of flying planes. Jessica Cox made her dream come true, despite being born without arms.

KEYWORD PROMPTS

Jessica Cox interview

SKULLS AND SKELETONS!

> **digit:** a finger or toe in a human, or a bone in the same location in another vertebrate. Also a number 0 through 9.
>
> **WORDS TO KNOW**

WHAT ARE YOUR DIGITS?

When skeleton scientists use the word *digit*, they are talking about the bones at the very end of animals' forelimbs and hind limbs. On humans, the digits are also known as fingers or toes. Digit is also a word used for the numbers 0 through 9. This is because people first started counting by using their fingers and toes. Being on the internet is called digital communication because computers use 0s and 1s to store and transport information. Can you think of other ways we use the word "digit?"

Bats have wings as their forelimbs and hands. The wings are made of the arm, wrist, and palm bones, plus five very long fingers. Birds' wings have three short fingers! Whales have flippers, which are like wings for the water. A finger in the flipper of a great blue whale can have up to eight bones! The front fins of fish are made of bony rays.

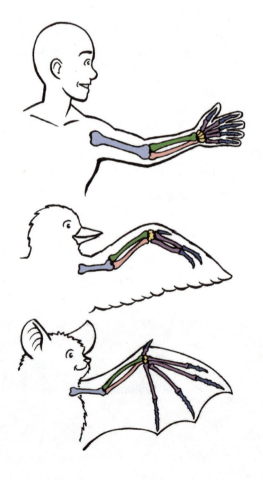

68

GIVE YOURSELF A HAND!

THESE FEET WERE MADE FOR WALKING

arch: a curved structure in the shape of an upside down U.

WORDS TO KNOW

Most four-legged animals don't have hands, wings, flippers, or fins at the end of their forelimbs. They have feet! A foot is the part of the body on which an animal stands. Feet are mostly used for getting an animal from one place to another. But what else can feet be used for?

Eagles catch fish and other animals with their feet. Gorillas have a thumb on each hind foot that lets them hold things. Badgers and moles have very long claws on their feet to help them dig holes in the soil.

DID YOU KNOW?

If you see an animal track in mud, snow, or sand, count the number of toes on each foot. This will give you a big clue to its identity.

Humans have a foot at the end of each hind limb. Each foot has 12 bones in the ankle and *arch*. The big toe has two bones, while the other four toes have three bones each.

Zebras, horses, and donkeys have only one toe on each foot. Balancing on one tippy toe on each foot helps these animals run faster. Why might their feet have adapted this way?

69

SKULLS AND SKELETONS!

SIGN LANGUAGE

You know what else bones can be good for? Communicating! Here's how you sign the letters for the word "love." The "L" is made by pointing your pointer finger straight up and your thumb straight out. The other three fingers are folded down. The letter "O" is made by connecting all your fingertips with your thumb to make a circle shape. The letter "V" looks like a peace sign, or bunny ears! The "E" is made by curling all your fingers together inward and connecting them with your thumb across the tips. L-O-V-E!

Ostriches, oxen, and camels have two toes on each foot. Many vertebrates have three, four, or five toes on each foot. In most vertebrates, all the toes point forward. But robins, cardinals, and other songbirds have three toes pointing forward and one toe pointing back. This helps them hold onto branches. Owls can move one toe from facing forward to facing backward to help it grab its prey.

You have learned a lot about all kinds of skulls and skeletons. But don't stop! Watch live animals around you to see skeletons in action. Clean and compare bones you find in the food you eat. Visit museums and compare skeletons on display. Look back through your journal to find questions you still want to explore.

You are on your way to becoming an awesome skeleton scientist!

? CONSIDER AND DISCUSS

It's time to consider and discuss: How many ways do you use your hands and feet?

PROJECT!

BONE SURVEY

SUPPLIES
- science journal and pencil
- ruler
- 2 male and 2 female friends or family members

Different animals have very different types of hands and feet. But the hands and feet of all people are alike—right? Let's find out!

1 Spread your fingers apart and place one hand on an empty page in your journal. Use the pencil to trace around it. Label it with your name.

2 Place one foot on another page and trace around it. Be sure to get the pencil between your toes!

3 Use the ruler to measure the length of each digit. Write the lengths on the drawing.

4 Repeat these steps for each other person. Look for patterns and record your observations before you read the notes below.

• **DID YOU KNOW?** •

The Statue of Liberty has Morton's feet!

THINK ABOUT IT!

Most boys have longer ring fingers than **index fingers**. Most girls have longer index fingers than ring fingers. Your big toe has two bones while your other toes have three each. If the end bone in your big toe is short, it will make your second toe look longer. This is called having a Morton's, or Greek, foot. If the big toe is longer, it is called an Egyptian foot. Your big toe is in line with your toes. Your thumb is off to one side. These differences are big! See why by doing the activity *You are All Thumbs!* on page 78!

WORDS TO KNOW

index finger: the finger closest to the thumb.

PROJECT!

GET A GRIP!

The pad of a bald eagle's foot is about 4 square inches. Each toe is between 1¼ and 2¼ inches long. When a bald eagle squeezes something with its foot, it is applying about 400 pounds of pressure for every inch. How well can you do?

SUPPLIES
- science journal and pencil
- bathroom or similar scale
- graph paper with 1-inch squares (www.math.kent.edu/~white/graphpaper/one-bold.pdf)
- calculator

1 Start a new page in your journal. Write this equation in your journal:

_____ ÷ _____ = _____
    A   B   C

In this equation, A = pounds of pressure, B = palm size, and C = pounds per square inch.

2 Place the scale on a flat surface. Use one hand to press down on the scale as hard as you can. But use only one hand! Record that number above line A in the equation.

FLEX THOSE FINGERS

What do rock climbers and guitar players have in common? They have very strong and flexible fingers. Rock climbers climb, hold, and sometimes even hang onto the sides of rock cliffs with just their fingers! Guitar players' fingers get stronger from making chords and strumming the strings. Can you think of other people who need strong fingers?

PROJECT!

3 Place the same hand on a piece of graph paper. Trace around it and color in the squares. Count the number of colored squares that are more than half colored. That is about the size of your hand in square inches. Write that number above line B in the equation.

4 Use your math skills or a calculator to divide A by B. The result (C) is the amount of pressure in pounds your hand can exert per square inch. Would you want to thumb wrestle an eagle?

TRY THIS! Repeat the activity for the other hand. Does one hand exert greater pressure than the other?

PROJECT!

MOVING AIR AND WATER

Birds and bats have wings that help them fly in the air. Dolphins and fish have fins that help them swim in the water. See how such finger adaptations help these animals to move faster with less work.

SUPPLIES
* flour
* digital camera or smartphone with video option (video optional)
* clear sandwich bag
* 2 towels
* clear plastic tub
* water
* red, blue, and yellow food color

Part 1: Wings Move Air

1 Sprinkle a light coating of flour on top of a table. Take a picture.

2 Spread your fingers apart. Hold them about 2 inches above a section of the flour. Wave this hand as fast as you can for 10 seconds. Take another picture of the table top.

3 Put your fingers together. Hold them about 2 inches above a different section of the flour. Wave this hand as fast as you can for 10 seconds. Take a picture of the table top.

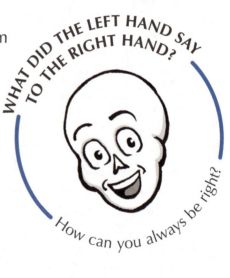

WHAT DID THE LEFT HAND SAY TO THE RIGHT HAND? How can you always be right?

4 Place the plastic bag over your hand. Spread your fingers apart. Hold them about 2 inches above another section of the flour. Wave this hand as fast as you can for 10 seconds. Take a picture of the table top.

5 What is different about each picture? Record your observations in your journal.

PROJECT!

Part 2: Flippers Move Water

1 Put one towel on a desk or table. Put the tub on the towel and fill it with water. If you have a video camera, place it at one end of the tub, where it won't fall in. Start filming at any time.

2 Add one drop of yellow food color to the center of the tub. Spread the fingers on one hand far apart. Put this hand in the middle of the tub. Slowly move it back and forth. What happens to the color? Take your hand out and dry it off.

3 Add one drop of red food color to the water. Keep the fingers of one hand close together. Put this hand in the middle of the tub. Slowly move it back and forth. Watch what happens to the color. How is it different from your first test? Take your hand out and dry it off.

4 Add one drop of blue food color to the center of the water. Place your fingers inside the plastic sandwich bag. Spread them apart. Place this hand in the water. Slowly move it back and forth. Watch what happens to the color. What do you notice?

THINK ABOUT IT! Ducks, geese, and some other birds have both wings and webbed feet. Why? Can you think of any mammals that live on both land and water?

PROJECT!

ARCH TEST

Human feet are a bit odd. The big toe is in line with the other foot bones. This lets human feet make arches between their toes and their heels. It helps humans push off with their toes. It also helps to reduce the force hitting the bones when the feet hit the ground.

SUPPLIES
- science journal and pencil
- ruler
- thin cardboard (cereal or cracker box works fine)
- scissors
- 2 bricks or blocks
- 50 pennies

1 Start a new page in your journal. Read through this project and start a scientific method worksheet. Write the question you are trying to answer at the top. What is your hypothesis?

2 Use the ruler and pencil to draw at least two strips on the cardboard that are 3 inches wide by 10 inches long. Cut out the strips.

3 Place the bricks on their sides about 3 inches apart. Make a bridge by laying one cardboard strip across the space to span the bricks.

4 Add one penny at a time to the middle of the paper bridge. Record how many pennies the strip can hold before it falls.

PROJECT!

5 Make an arch between the bricks using one strip. Place a second strip over the top.

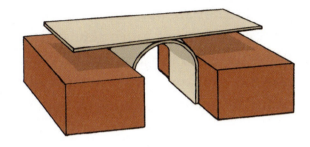

6 Add one penny at a time to the middle. Record how many pennies the strip arch can hold.

7 Move the bricks closer together and try your experiment, then farther apart and try it. What is the strongest size for this arch?

TRY IT! A fun way to compare foot arches is to make wet footprints on a sidewalk or piece of paper. The arched part of the foot will not show up, because it does not touch the ground. Take pictures of the footprints or measure how long and wide the dry spot (arch) is on each one.

AWESOME, AMAZING ARCHES

Look around. You can see arches in bridges, tunnels, dams, and sports arenas. Like the arch in a human foot, builders use arches to help spread the weight pushing down off to the sides. Some arch bridges built in Greece around 1300 BCE are still standing and being used.

PROJECT!

YOU ARE ALL THUMBS!

Your thumbs are **opposable**. This means the tip of your thumb can touch almost all parts of every other finger on the same hand. A thumb that can move in so many ways is very useful! How many things do you do that need an opposable thumb?

SUPPLIES
* science journal and pencil
* timer
* tape
* string or yarn
* shirt with buttons
* Ziploc bag
* bottle with screw top
* tweezers

1 In your science journal, make a table like the one below.

Action	Opposable thumb time	Taped thumb time
Pick up a pencil and write your name		
Tie a knot in the string		
Button and unbutton shirt		
Open and zip close a Ziploc bag		
Uncap and recap a bottle		
Cut off a piece of masking tape		
Pick up a pencil using tweezers		

WORDS TO KNOW

opposable: capable of being placed against one or more digits of the same hand or foot.

PROJECT!

2 Record how long it takes to do each task with your normal hands.

3 Have a friend or adult tape your thumbs to the sides of your hands. Repeat all the tasks, recording how long they take to do with taped thumbs.

> **THINK ABOUT IT!** Animals with opposable toes walk with flat feet. They cannot run as fast as humans. But they use their toes to hang onto things, which makes them much better at climbing trees! What everyday tasks do humans need a thumb to do?

DID YOU KNOW?

Other animals have opposable digits as well. Giant pandas, koalas, macaques, gibbons, and even some tree frogs have opposable digits on their front limbs. Opossums have opposable digits on their hind feet. And gorillas, orangutans, bonobos, and chimpanzees have opposable digits on both their front limbs and hind feet.

PROJECT!

SIMPLY SYMMETRICAL SKELETON

Imagine there was a line starting between your eyes and going all the way down your trunk. Each side of the skeleton has the same parts. It looks like a mirror image, or symmetrical! Use this idea to make a skeleton model.

SUPPLIES
- 5 sheets copy paper
- pencil
- scissors
- ruler
- white rectangle foam tray
- tape or glue

1 Fold two sheets of copy paper in half the short way. Cut them along the center line.

2 Fold one of the cut pieces in half again. Draw half a skull along the crease.

3 Keeping the paper folded, cut out the face and open it up. Repeat these steps to make hands and feet.

4 Cut three sheets of copy paper into 22 to 24 strips that are about 2 inches wide. Glue or tape the ends of four strips to make rings.

5 The foam tray is the trunk of your skeleton. Use the glue or tape to attach the head to one end of the tray.

WORDS TO KNOW

symmetrical: the same on both sides or ends.

PROJECT!

6 Attach one ring at each corner of the tray to start your arms and legs. Make paper chains by adding one strip at a time to each ring. The arm chains should be at least one ring shorter than the leg chains.

7 Finish by adding the hands and feet to the ends.

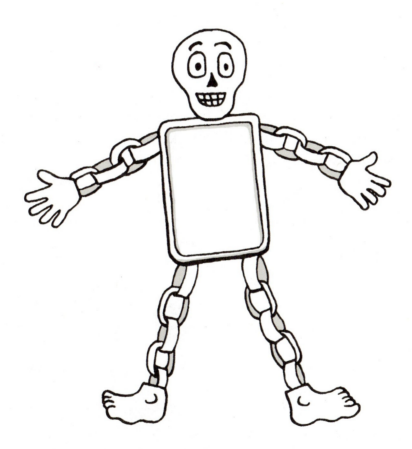

TRY THIS! Make a skeleton model of a different animal! How is your animal different? How is it similar?

PROJECT!

CELEBRATE SKULLS

People around the world use skulls for decorations. It's easy to make a re-usable skull that does double duty as a night light! Sleep tight!

> **SUPPLIES**
> * empty plastic milk jug
> * paint or permanent markers
> * glow stick

1 Soak an empty plastic milk jug in warm water so the label is easy to remove. Rinse it out and let it dry.

2 While the jug is drying, think about your skull design. Is the mouth of the jug the mouth of your skull or where the vertebrae are attached? Is the handle a crest on the top of the skull, a big nose, or a hyoid bone at the bottom?

3 Once the jug is dry, use the paint or markers to draw skull parts—eye sockets and more!

4 When you want the skull to be on display, unwrap and snap a glow stick. Shake it a few times so the color spreads. Put it in your skull and admire your work!

TRY THIS! Use your skull lantern with your carved pumpkins for Halloween.

GLOSSARY

acid: a sour-tasting liquid that dissolves some minerals.

adaptation: something about a plant or animal that helps it survive.

adapt: to make changes to better survive in an environment.

amphibian: a cold-blooded vertebrate animal, such as a toad, frog, or salamander. Amphibians live on land and in the water.

anatomy: the body parts of an animal.

antler: on the heads of some animals in the deer family, a bony point that is shed.

aquatic: having to do with water.

arch: a curved structure in the shape of an upside down U.

balance point: the spot on a beam where the weight is equal on each side.

BCE: put after a date, BCE stands for Before Common Era and counts down to zero. CE stands for Common Era and counts up from zero. These nonreligious terms correspond to BC and AD. This book was printed in 2019 CE.

bird: a warm-blooded vertebrate animal with feathers covering most of its body. Birds hatch from eggs and most have wings that help them fly. Turkeys, ducks, and penguins are birds.

blood vessel: a thin tube in an animal's body through which blood travels.

bone: hard, connective tissue in an animal's body that provides support, protection and a place for muscle attachment. Blood is produced in some bones.

breaking point: the place at which something can no longer stay together.

cartilage: elastic, flexible tissue in the body.

cell: the basic part of a living thing. Cells are so small they can be seen only with a microscope. There are billions of cells in most living things.

classify: to put things in groups based on what they have in common.

cold-blooded: an animal whose body temperature changes with the air or water temperature around it.

cranium: the part of the skull that encloses the brain.

crest: a tuft or ridge on top of a head or hill.

digit: a finger or toe in a human, or a bone in the same location in another vertebrate. Also a number 0 through 9.

dislocate: to displace a bone from normal connections with another bone.

dissect: to cut something apart to study what is inside.

dissolve: when a solid becomes an invisible part of a liquid.

dominance: being the leader because of greater strength.

evaporate: to convert from a liquid to a gas.

evolve: to gradually develop through time.

exoskeleton: a hard shell or cover on the outside of some invertebrates that provides support and protection.

femur: the upper bone in a hind limb.

fibula: one of the thin bones between the femur and the ankle.

fish: a vertebrate animal that lives in water, uses gills to breathe, and usually hatches from an egg. Fish do not have any limbs and most have scales. Goldfish, eels, and sharks are fish.

SKULLS AND SKELETONS!

forelimb: the arms, legs, wings, flippers, or fins on a vertebrate that are attached closest to the head.

fossil: the remains of any organism, including animals and plants, that have been preserved in rock.

fracture: a broken bone.

fuse: to join together.

harvest: to pick or gather something.

hind limb: the legs that are attached closest to the tail end of a vertebrate.

horizontal: straight across from side to side.

horn: on the heads of some animals, a permanent point with a bony core covered with keratin.

humerus: the arm bone between the shoulder and elbow.

hyoid: the bone in your throat at the base of your tongue.

index finger: the finger closest to the thumb.

invertebrate: an animal that does not have bones inside its body.

joint: the movable place where two or more bones meet.

keel: a bony ridge on the center line of a bird's sternum.

keratin: a protein that forms fingernails, beaks, hair, feathers, and claws.

lever: a bar that is used to lift a heavy load.

ligament: the tough, stretchy tissue that connects two or more bones together.

limb: a part of a vertebrate's skeleton that is mostly used for movement.

mammal: a warm-blooded vertebrate animal, such as a human, dog, or cat. Mammals feed milk to their young and usually have hair or fur covering most of their skin.

mandible: the lower jaw bone.

marrow: a jelly-like goo in the middle of some larger bones where new blood cells are made.

minerals: the natural ingredients that are part of all things on Earth. Salt and calcium are examples of minerals.

nerves: living fibers that carry information between the brain and the rest of the body.

nostrils: the one or two holes in a skull that bring air in and out and smells into the body.

opposable: capable of being placed against one or more digits of the same hand or foot.

organ: a part of the body, such as the heart or lungs, that performs a certain function inside the body.

organ system: a group of tissues in a living body that work together to do a specific job.

palate: the roof of the mouth.

paralyzed: unable to move.

patella: the kneecap.

pelvis: the large bony structure near the end of a vertebrate's backbone where the hind limbs attach.

predator: an animal that hunts and eats other animals.

prey: an animal that gets hunted and eaten by another animal.

primate: any member of the group of mammals that includes humans, monkeys, and apes.

GLOSSARY

protractor: a device for drawing and measuring angles.

radius: one of the thin bones between the humerus and wrist.

reptile: a cold-blooded vertebrate animal such as a snake, lizard, alligator, or turtle, that has a spine, lays eggs, has scales or horny plates, and breathes air.

rib cage: the bony box in the chest of vertebrates that is made mostly of ribs. It protects the heart and lungs.

rodent: the group of mammals that use their ever-growing front teeth to chew on things. Rodents make up more than half of all mammals on Earth and include mice, rats, squirrels, chipmunks, beavers, and gerbils.

sacrum: a triangular bone in the lower back that is located between the two hipbones of the pelvis.

salvage: to pick up and save something that would otherwise be destroyed.

scapula: a shoulder blade.

simulate: to imitate certain conditions for the purpose of testing or study.

skeleton: the framework of bones that supports the body of a vertebrate animal.

skull: the bone case that holds in place and protects the brain and other parts of an animal's head.

species: a group of animals that is different in some way from all other groups of animals.

spine: a line of connected bones called vertebrae that runs down the back of an animal with bones. Also known as a backbone.

stem cell: a self-renewing cell that divides to create cells with the potential to become specialized cells.

sternum: the flat bone that connects the top ribs in some vertebrates.

symmetrical: the same on both sides or ends.

tendon: the tough, stretchy tissue that connects muscles to bones.

tibia: one of the thin bones between the femur and the ankle.

tissue: a group or mass of similar cells working together to perform common functions in plants and animals.

torso: the human body except the head, arms, and legs.

ulna: one of the thin bones between the humerus and wrist.

upright: sitting or standing with the back in a vertical line.

vertebrae: the small bones that form the backbone.

vertebrate: any animal that has a spine.

vertical: straight up and down.

vision: the ability to see things using your eyes.

volume: the amount of space an object takes up.

warm-blooded: an animal that can create its own body heat.

X-ray: a powerful wave of energy that lets doctors see bones inside bodies.

SKULLS AND SKELETONS!

BOOKS

Artell, Mike. *Skulls*. MJA Creative, 2015.

Barner, Bob. *Sea Bones*. Chronicle Books, 2015.

Colson, Rob Scott. *Bone Collection: Animals*. Scholastic Press, 2013.

de la Bedoyere, Camilla. *Bone Collection: Skulls*. Scholastic Press, 2014.

Hewitt, Sally. *Your Bones: Science in Action*. QEB Publishing, 2016.

MUSEUMS

Many natural history museums have at least some skulls and skeletons on display. This listing includes some museums where skulls and skeletons are featured exhibits.

Beneski Museum of Natural History, Amherst, Massachusetts:
amherst.edu/museums/naturalhistory/collections/osteology

Biodiversity Institute and Natural History Museum, Lawrence, Kansas:
biodiversity.ku.edu/exhibits/mammal-skulls

California Academy of Natural Science, San Francisco, California:
calacademy.org/exhibits/skulls

Hall of Bones, Smithsonian Institute, Washington, DC:
si.edu/Exhibitions/Osteology-Hall-of-Bones-137

Museum of Osteology, Oklahoma City, Oklahoma, and Orlando, Florida:
skeletonmuseum.com

ESSENTIAL QUESTIONS

Introduction: What do you think are the largest bones in your body?

Chapter 1: What would your body be like without bones?

Chapter 2: Why do some vertebrates have parts on their heads that humans don't have?

Chapter 3: How does having an upright body change a skeleton?

Chapter 4: Which are longer and stronger, your arms or your legs? How can you tell?

Chapter 5: How many ways do you use your hands and feet?

RESOURCES

QR CODE GLOSSARY

Page 5: news.nationalgeographic.com/news/2012/01/120111-smallest-frogs-vertebrates-new-species-science-animals

Page 13: guinnessworldrecords.com/world-records/largest-external-foot-rotation

Page 28: skullsite.com.transurl.nl/3d-models

Page 33: sporcle.com/games/cbdollyy/animalskullsmatching

Page 37: instructables.com/id/How-to-do-a-Forensic-Facial-Reconstruction

Page 53: seewinter.com/animals/webcams/winter-zone-cam-1

Page 59: kidwings.com/virtual-pellet

Page 60: youtube.com/watch?v=5VJTtxQ8kks

Page 67: youtube.com/watch?v=fK0LvmurKbU

METRIC CONVERSIONS

Use this chart to find the metric equivalents to the English measurements in this book. If you need to know a half measurement, divide by two. If you need to know twice the measurement, multiply by two. How do you find a quarter measurement? How do you find three times the measurement?

English	Metric
1 inch	2.5 centimeters
1 foot	30.5 centimeters
1 yard	0.9 meter
1 mile	1.6 kilometers
1 pound	0.5 kilogram
1 teaspoon	5 milliliters
1 tablespoon	15 milliliters
1 cup	237 milliliters

SKULLS AND SKELETONS!

A

Achilles tendon, 13
activities (Project!)
  Any Body?, 8–9
  Arch Test, 76–77
  Balancing Act, 52–53
  Bone Building, 50
  Bone Hard!, 18–19
  Bone Survey, 71
  Celebrate Skulls, 82
  Easy X-Ray, 24–25
  Edible Bones, 22–23
  Elastic Girl!, 20–21
  Get a Grip!, 72–73
  How Big Is the Brain?, 36
  Limbs as Levers, 62–63
  Look Around!, 40–41
  Measuring Up!, 64–65
  Moving Air and Water, 74–75
  Muscle Model, 61
  Perfect Protection, 34–35
  Putting It All Together!, 51
  Rock Face, 37
  Simply Symmetrical Skeleton, 80–81
  Skulls and Skeletons Science Journal, 7
  Spool Spine, 48–49
  Vision Test, 38–39
  You Are All Thumbs!, 78–79
amphibians, 3, 15, 27, 29–30, 43–44, 58–59
animals
  invertebrate, 5, 9, 27
  vertebrate, 2–5, 8–9, 10–25, 26–41, 42–53, 54–65, 66–82
ankles, iv, 58, 69
antlers, 31–32
Aristotle, iv
arm bones, 3–4, 54–65. *See also* hands; wrists

B

ball and socket joints, 14, 46
birds, 3, 15, 27–30, 32, 40, 43–47, 54–55, 58–59, 68–70, 72, 74–75
blood, 4, 11, 56
bone marrow, v, 4, 12
bones
  average number of, 15, 27, 32, 66, 67, 69
  broken or damaged, iv–v, 12, 56
  collection or display of, v, 16, 23
  connections between, 4, 13–14, 43, 44, 47, 54, 61
  definition of, 1, 10
  diseases of, v, 21
  eating or chewing on, 22, 59
  fossilized, 45
  fused, 12, 23, 46, 48, 58
  growth or maturation of, 12, 50
  in hands and feet, 3, 14, 17, 58, 66–79
  hardening of, 10–12, 18–21
  in history, iv–v, 15–17
  jobs or functions of, 3–5, 26, 34, 42–43, 67, 69
  in limbs, 3–4, 54–65. *See also* feet; hands
  muscles and, iv, 3, 13, 26, 29, 31, 44–45, 48, 50, 61
  skull, iv, 3, 12, 26–32, 34–41, 82
  in torso, 2, 3, 14, 42–53, 54–55. *See also* spine or backbone

C

calcium, 11–12, 18–19, 21, 22, 56
carpals, 68. *See also* wrists
cartilage, 4, 11, 28
cells, v, 4–5, 10–12, 18, 56
collarbones, 43, 54
Cope, Edward Drinker, 51
Cox, Jessica, 67
craniums, 30–32
CT/CAT scans, 25

INDEX

D

Daubenton, Louis Jean Marie, v
Da Vinci, Leonardo, iv
Day, Maxwell, 13
digits, 68. *See also* fingers; toes
diseases, v, 21

E

ear bones, 3, 12
essential questions, 6, 17, 33, 47, 60, 70
exoskeletons, 5, 9
eyes, 30, 38–41

F

feet, 3, 14, 58, 66–67, 68, 69–72, 76–77, 79
femur, 57
fibula, 57
fingers, 14, 66–68, 70–72, 78–79
fins, 3, 46, 54–55, 74, 75
fish, 3, 15, 27, 29–30, 46, 54–55, 68, 74–75
flippers, 54–55, 68, 75
forelimbs, 54, 58–59, 67–68. *See also* arm bones; hands
fossils, 45
funny bone, 58
fused bones, 12, 23, 46, 48, 58

G

Galen, iv
growth plates, 12

H

hands, 3, 14, 17, 58, 66–68, 70–75, 78–79
hind limbs, 55, 58–59, 68. *See also* feet; leg bones
hinge joints, 14
Hippocrates, iv
hips, 3, 14, 46, 48
horns, 31–32
humerus, 56, 68
Hunter, John, iv
hyoid bone, 4, 33

I

invertebrates, 5, 9, 27

J

jaws, 29, 32
joints, 13–14, 46. *See also* hips; knees; shoulders
journal, science, 6, 7

K

knees, iv, 14, 55, 57

L

leg bones, 3–4, 54–65. *See also* ankles; feet; knees
ligaments, 13
limbs, bones in, 3–4, 54–65. *See also* feet; hands

M

mammals, 3, 15, 27–32, 43–44, 46–47, 54–60, 66–79
Mapp, Sally, v
measurements, 65
metacarpals, 68
minerals, 4–5, 11–12, 18–19, 21, 22, 45, 56, 59
movement or motion, 3, 13–14, 29, 40–41, 44, 45–46, 54–55, 58–63, 69, 74–77
MRIs, 25
muscles, iv, 3, 13, 26, 29, 31, 44–45, 48, 50, 61

N

necks, 32–33, 40–41, 48
noses, 28

SKULLS AND SKELETONS!

P

palates, 32
patella, 57
Peeper, Jeannie, v
pelvis, 43, 46, 55
phalanges, 68. *See also* fingers; toes
pivot joints, 14

R

radius, 56, 68
reptiles, 3, 15, 27, 29–32, 43–44, 46–47, 54–55, 59–60
ribs/rib cage, 2, 3, 43, 44, 46
rickets, 21
Roentgen, Wilhelm, v, 17

S

sacrum, 48
saddle joints, 14
shoulder blades or scapulae, 15, 43, 45, 54
shoulders, 3, 14
sign language, 70
skeleton, iv–v, 4, 5, 8–9, 16, 51, 80–81. *See also* bones
skulls, iv, 3, 12, 26–32, 34–41, 82
sliding joints, 14
spine or backbone, 1–3, 4, 8–9, 12–13, 32–33, 43, 44–46, 48–49
stem cells, v
sternum, 43, 44–45

T

tails/tailbones, 2, 46–47, 48, 52–53, 59
teeth, 29
tendons, 13, 57
Thomas, E. Donnall, v
Thomas, Hugh Owen, v
thumbs, 14, 65, 67, 69, 70, 71, 78–79
tibia, 57
timeline, iv–v
toes, 14, 66, 68, 69–72, 79
torso, bones in, 2, 3, 14, 42–53, 54–55. *See also* spine or backbone

U

ulna, 56, 68

V

Venel, Jean-Andre, v
vertebrae, 32–33, 43, 44–46, 48–49. *See also* spine or backbone
vertebrates, 2–5, 8–9, 10–25, 26–41, 42–53, 54–65, 66–82
Vesalius, Andreas, iv
vitamin D, 21

W

wings, 3, 44, 54, 58–59, 68, 74
wrists, 14, 58, 67–68

X

X-rays, v, 17, 24–25, 67